EXPERT PROFILES

VOLUME 5

Conversations with Influencers & Innovators

EXPERT PROFILES
VOLUME 5
Conversations with Influencers & Innovators

Featuring

Joel Hawbaker

James Hsieh (JH)

Adam Vest

Jim Yeargan

Dan Goldstein

Fiona Johnson

Dr. Paul S. Inselman

Shawna Ranae

Lefford Fate

Brandy Sales

Royalties from the Retail Sales of "Expert Profiles" are
donated to Global Autism Project

AUTISM KNOWS **NO BORDERS;**
FORTUNATELY NEITHER DO WE.®

Global Autism Project 501(c)3, is a nonprofit organization which provides training to local individuals in evidence-based practices for individuals with autism.

Global Autism Project believes that every child has the ability to learn and their potential should not be limited by geographical bounds.

The Global Autism Project seeks to eliminate the disparity in service provision seen around the world by providing high-quality training to individuals providing services in their local community. This training is made sustainable through regular training trips and contiguous remote training.

You can learn more about Global Autism Project by visiting GlobalAutismProject.org.

Table of Contents

Joel Hawbaker – Confident Humility 1

James Hsieh (JH) – CEO and Internet Business
Consultant (a.k.a. The Marketing Jedi)...................................15

Adam Vest – How to Maximize Digital Marketing for
Service-Based Businesses...33

Jim Yeargan – What to do if You Get Pulled Over
for DUI..51

Dan Goldstein – How to Attract More Leads for Doctors,
Attorneys and Dentists..67

Fiona Johnson – Empowering Leaders to Release
Ineffective Patterns and Habits for Greater Success..............83

Dr. Paul S. Inselman – Helping Business Owners Create
Financial Freedom Through Marketing...................................97

Shawna Ranae – Entrepreneur | Visionary
| Philanthropist 109

Lefford Fate – Working with Military Veterans
Transitioning into Civilian Life 133

Brandy Sales – Make $1K per Day with
Smartphone Video 147

Confident Humility

In addition to speaking on leadership, blended family life, and education, Joel is an award-winning high school teacher and soccer coach. He recently self-published a book titled *Inverted Leadership: Lead Others Better by Forgetting About Yourself,* and he is also involved in helping teach leadership classes at Duke University's Summer Studies program for gifted high school students.

Conversation with Joel Hawbaker

Give us a little bit of a background on yourself and how you came to start Real Life Leading.

Joel Hawbaker: Certainly. I'm a high school history and Bible teacher, and I coach high school soccer as well. I'm also divorced and remarried. I've got two daughters, and so a large part of what I focus on in working with kids is teaching them how to have better relationships. A lot of that comes from my own world in terms of coming from a divorced home and then also going through a divorce as an adult in my mid-20s. So, my goal is to help other people have better relationships and lead themselves better so that they can also lead other people better. Part of that is because I've seen it done well. Part of that is I've made plenty of mistakes and I'd love to help other people avoid them.

Have you found when you're working with, or speaking to, groups, it just seems to click for them because they have resonated with something that you've gone through yourself?

Joel Hawbaker: Absolutely. I think that's one of the things that really helps. I teach high school, and given the divorce rate today, over half the kids that I teach come from divorced homes or they come from blended families. Because I teach at a small Christian school, a lot of times with kids, there's this perception that if you're a high school teacher and you teach at a Christian school, you've never known anything but Christianity and all you've ever done is have a perfect, easy life, and that's why you're a teacher in a Christian school. When I tell them, "My parents split up when I was in middle school and then I went through a divorce when I was in my mid to late 20s. Now, I'm remarried, and my ex-wife is remarried, and we have a blended family because my kids have a stepdad and a stepmom, and they have a little brother at their mom's house, and this is our world." Kids kind of go, "Oh, so you have an idea of where I'm coming from." It helps me make a connection with them. It also helps me make a connection with other adults who have been through it. And unfortunately, the church sometimes has gained a reputation of being less welcoming to people who have made mistakes, and so part of my goal is to help people realize that everybody has made mistakes. It's been said that "The church should not be a museum for saints. It should be a hospital for sinners."

When I went through my divorce, the people I relied on were my immediate family, but also my church family, because that's where you need to go when you're hurting, when you're broken. Church is where you need to be even more. If the church isn't accepting people who have made mistakes, then who is? So that's one of the things I like to talk about, to remind people that what we ought to be doing is learning from our mistakes and then openly, humbly sharing our mistakes to help other people avoid them.

I would obviously love for both of my daughters grow up and get married and stay married to the same person until they're 110 years old! I would love that. And so how do I try to teach them to do better than I did? By being open and honest about my mistakes.

Right! Why not just be transparent? Because people know it anyway, correct?

Joel Hawbaker: That's right, and kids, especially high school kids, are quick to see through a faker. They might not know exactly what you're faking, but they're good at telling when you're not genuine. And so again, like you said, it's easier to be transparent, but more importantly, it's just more honest. Just be genuine. Be open. Obviously, use a little bit of discretion. Don't tell them every single detail about every mistake you've ever made, but be honest. I do the same thing in my speaking.

You mentioned my business, I call it "Real Life Leading," and the reason for that is because whether it's in the home, in a business, in a relationship, or in a volunteer organization, the truth is most of us aren't going to be corporate CEOs or military commanders or professional sports coaches or athletes. Most of us aren't going to be that. Most of us are what I call "real life people." Real-life people are moms and dads, and they are small business owners, or they are mid-level management people, or they are youth group volunteers, or Sunday school teachers, or civic organization volunteers.

Your leadership in those positions is every bit as important. In fact, in my book, I argue that the smaller your audience is, the more important your leadership, because you're going to have a bigger impact on a smaller audience. That's not to knock a CEO of a company with 5,000 employees. A CEO is obviously important. They live or die by their decisions because they affect 5,000 people.

But I also know that I have more impact on my two daughters than I do on my 30 soccer players. I spend more time with them. I spend more one on one time with them. And because of that, I have a bigger impact on the smaller audience. So that means, I need to make sure that regardless of the size of my audience, that my leadership is consistent, that it's honest, that it is integrity based, and that we are pursuing the correct thing.

So, you need to know how to lead enough and know it down pat so well that when "real life" pops up and rears its ugly head you can just bob-and-weave and not get thrown for a loop. How does one do that?

Joel Hawbaker: Absolutely. That's a great question. I think a lot of it goes back to first, self-awareness. You must know who you are and what you believe and what you stand for. Because I love the military saying, "You don't rise to the occasion, you sink to the level of your training." And CS Lewis talks about that in his book *Mere Christianity*; he says something like, "Circumstances don't shape our character; they reveal the character that's already there." He uses an analogy about if you walk into a basement and turn the light on quickly, you're going to see the rats. But turning the light on didn't create the rats. They were already there.

And so, the idea there is that we need to know who we are, and what we believe in, and what we stand for. Because in the moments when our values are tested, that's what we're going to fall back on. And then it becomes a question: how much do you really believe what you say you believe? And so, for me, everything starts with humility: every aspect of leadership as a husband, as a father, as a teacher, as a coach, as an author, as a speaker, in my world, everything I do needs to start with humility. And that's a word that for me is drastically misunderstood in the English language, unfortunately.

A lot of people think that humility is synonymous with modesty or weakness. That may be humility, but a lot of times it's just dishonesty.

Do you mean if that person played down their skill, then they could be preventing someone else from being impacted positively?

Joel Hawbaker: That's exactly it. And my book about that is called, *Inverted Leadership: Lead Others Better by Forgetting About Yourself.* The way that I explain that is, people misunderstand confidence and they confuse it with arrogance. Confidence is just simply being sure of what your gifts are.

And that's really all it is. It's not shying away from them, but it's also not going out of your way to toot your own horn. The way that I help distinguish that, I borrow a lot from CS Lewis's *Mere Christianity.* He says that, "The way that you can tell confidence from pride is that pride is inherently and always competitive." A confident person, like in my position, I would say, "I know that I'm a good high school teacher, and a good soccer coach. I have years of experience, a lot of training, and the results are pretty clear." A prideful person would simply say, "I'm a better teacher than that guy," or "I'm a better coach than that guy." And that's why I mean pride is inherently competitive. Because the other guy doesn't have this; whether it's the results or the technique. But with pride, a person has to *compare* themselves based on something. And again, CS Lewis says, that the prideful person is never content with what they have, they're just always worried about having more than you.

What is "Confident Humility"?

Joel Hawbaker: I say that it is being sure of what your gifts are and then using those gifts in the service of other people. As I mentioned before, CS Lewis tells us "Humility is not thinking less of yourself, it's thinking of yourself less." Okay. That means leaders need to be asking themselves, "What am I good at and how can I use that to benefit other people?" Because to me, the absolute crucial component of good leadership is taking your own desires out of the equation, and then asking yourself what you would do.

Because if I take my ego out of it, my teaching looks different because now I have a lot more patience when kids ask questions that I would find ridiculous or when my soccer players don't want to do something that I want and that inconveniences me. Because let's be honest, in our personal lives, most of the time when we get upset, it's not when something giant happens. People understand when we're upset when we have a giant catastrophe. What really happens more often is that we get upset and fly off the handle when we are minorly inconvenienced. That's when we damage relationships as leaders. That's when we make big mistakes.

Think about how many times you've been driving to work, and somebody cuts you off and you get furious about it and it ruins the whole first half of your day. Well, that's just pride. That's, "I don't like it that you've cut me off in traffic, so I'm going to take it out on everybody around me." Well, that's poor leadership, and I'll fully admit, when I was younger, man, I was the world's best at that, and when I realized how much damage that was causing to relationships, that was when I started asking myself the question, "Okay. What's really at play here?" Do I have a right to be upset when someone cuts me off? Well, sure, but only if I'm taking it personally. They didn't cut me off because I'm me. They cut me off because they're in a hurry, they weren't paying attention, or a million other reasons. Just let it go.

Then there is the idea of the difference between success and impact, because ultimately, every leader is going to have to decide based on one of those two things, and whether you realize it or not, we are making decisions based on those things. The problem is most of the time, we make decisions based on being a success.

Now, you can define that in a million different ways. It might be getting a certain promotion or having a certain base salary or certain position or title. Whatever your definition of success is, it's not a bad thing to pursue success, but if you pursue success as its own end, a lot of times, it leaves people feeling empty. There's a famous actor a couple years ago who came out and said, "I wish everybody could be rich and famous and have everything they ever desired, and then that would help them realize that it doesn't satisfy." I think it was Jim Carrey that said something along those lines.

So, the question is, if success as its own end isn't good enough, what should we be doing? And my answer to that is *focusing on making a positive impact on the people around you*, because if you do that, you will be a success. So, for me, what that looks like as a high school coach is that I don't try to focus on winning soccer games. I used to, and because of that I made some coaching mistakes, meaning that I told players to do things on the soccer field they probably shouldn't have, and it wasn't necessarily cheating, but it also wasn't playing within the fair spirit of the game, you know what I mean? Everybody who's an athlete knows there's a gray area of, "Is that cheating?" Well, it's not really against the rules, but it's also not very sportsmanlike.

When I was younger, I was very ego-driven. Especially as a very young coach, you want to make a name for yourself, so you really want to win whatever you can win, and I did some of that. I told players to do stuff that, it wasn't illegal, but it also wasn't really sportsmanlike. When I look back at that, I'm ashamed of that, because especially as an outspoken Christian coaching mostly at Christian high schools, that's a terrible testimony.

I want to focus on making a positive impact on my students because, ultimately, my soccer players are not going to make a living from soccer. Very few people make a living as a professional athlete or a coach, but every kid I coach is going to be a human being for decades. I need to teach them how to be better people, not just better soccer players. We're still going to learn soccer. Praise the Lord, I've been blessed. We've got a great soccer program. The school I've been at the past five years, two of the last three years, we've been to our state championship game. We lost both and that kind of stunk, but at the same time, three or four years ago, we had never won a playoff game. In two years, we went from never winning a playoff game to going to back-to-back state championship games. Well, that's really great success, but at this point, those trophies are two or three years old, they're collecting dust in a trophy case, and almost every one of those kids has graduated.

So, what difference does it make now? Well, the answer is if I've taught them to be good people and if those kids are working or in college or in the military and they're having a positive impact on the world around them, now we're a success. Forget the trophies. So, self-leadership, helping improve personal development yourself, allows you to make a bigger impact on others.

What would you say is one thing that someone could do, immediately, when walking away from one of your presentations to get some quick impact?

One of the major takeaways is to just take five minutes and examine your three to five closest relationships and ask yourself a couple of questions about them. Ask yourself: "What am I giving in this relationship and how can I do better at that?" And, "Are there ways that I could be better serving these people around me? Are there ways that I could be helping them that maybe they haven't even thought of? What are some of the things I could do to help them out?"

I'm married. I've got kids. And so, for me, what that looks like is, how am I taking care of my wife? Am I serving her? Am I being a spiritual leader in our home? Am I making sure that her needs and desires and wants are met? And if I am, great. How can I improve on that? And if I'm not, what do I need to change tonight? So, for me, again, and I've really seen this in the past few years, I love sports. I could come home every day and immediately turn on soccer or baseball and basketball and just watch it all night, but the truth of the matter is that that would not be taking good care of my family, and one of the ways I know that to be true is because in my first marriage, I did do that when my kids were younger. I missed out on hours of interaction with my daughters when they were toddlers because I was too busy watching basketball or soccer games on TV. I would love to have that time back, but I can't, and so what that means is that now I want to really be conscious of how I spend my time, because again, I'm divorced and remarried. My kids go back and forth between my house and their mom's house each week, so I only get my kids half the time.

That means when my kids are with me, my kids and my wife need to be my Number One priority. As an example, high school soccer season for me is in the spring, so it's basically January to May, and what that looks like is, my younger daughter's birthday is in February and my wife's birthday is in January. Well, I do not schedule soccer games on my daughter's birthday, and I do not even go to soccer practice on my wife's birthday. My assistant coach does the coaching. My kids all know on January 8th, Coach Hawbaker will not be at practice because he's going home to see his wife. On February 19th, Coach Hawbaker will not be at practice. We will not have a game that day. It's his daughter's birthday. He's going to go where his daughter is.

I didn't do that my first year at the new high school, but I've done it every year since then, and it's something that I don't ever want to change because I need my kids to know that I love them, that I prioritize them, even over my job, and I tell my high school players, "Listen. It's not that I don't love you, but I want you to also prioritize your families."

We had a girl last year who has on our JV team. She dressed out with our varsity team sometimes, but her family was planning a trip. Her and her mom and her aunt and her sister, they were all going to travel for four days in the spring. It meant she was going to miss a soccer game, and she said, "Well, Coach, what do I do?" I said, "Go and have a great time. You may not ever have this opportunity again. How many games have you already had this year? Go on the trip, because you need to spend time with your family. You're going to be a daughter, a sister, a niece, your whole life. Go on the trip and have a great time, and we'll be here when you get back."

Again, it's not because I'm great. It's because I've done that poorly in my own world, so my encouragement to people would be, examine the closest relationships to you. Ask yourself what you could do better in those things, in those relationships. Even just today. Even if it's something little, like, after dinner, saying, "You know what, honey? I'll clean up the kitchen," or coming home and immediately turning your work phone off and putting it away for two hours so that you're not constantly getting text messages. Just something little like that. Go home and make sure that you're taking care of your family. Make sure that you're taking care of your team at work. Go to work and just ask a question, "Hey, what could I do differently this day that's going to help you do your job better?", as opposed to walking and saying, "Here's what I expect you to do because I think this will make you do your job better." You might be right, but if you ask them, they may have told you that, and now they're going to be even more on your side because you asked for their feedback.

If people were interested in bringing you in to speak with their school or their group or at a conference, what's the best way that they can reach out and learn more about you and make a connection?

The easiest way to get in touch with me is to come to my website www.reallifeleading.com, and you can email me there. You can connect with me on Twitter (@RealLifeleading), on Facebook (Facebook.com/RealLifeLeading), or on LinkedIn (Joel Hawbaker).

About Joel Hawbaker

Joel W. Hawbaker is a high school history/Bible teacher and soccer coach in Alabama, where he lives with his wife, his two daughters, and their two rescue dogs. He is also a speaker and the author of the book 'Inverted Leadership: Lead Others Better by Forgetting About Yourself.' Joel has a degree in history from Covenant College, and he has been studying leadership since his days as a student there.

Come by www.reallifeleading.com to sign up and get your free copy of my e-book *(Extra)Ordinary Leadership: 10 Things Dad Taught Me Without Saying Anything* as well as to get our weekly newsletter and blog posts on leadership.

CEO and Internet Business Consultant (a.k.a. The Marketing Jedi)

James Hsieh is CEO of Cybertegic, a seasoned digital marketing agency in Los Angeles that specializes in internet marketing and website development.

The success of his previous work in Nestlé back in 1998 led to an avenue of untapped opportunities and the birth of new dreams. In 2002, during the booming era of the Internet and e-commerce, James founded Cybertegic with a few partners to help small and mid-size businesses grow their businesses online.

Over the years, Cybertegic became an authority in various fields of digital marketing, such as Google Search Engine Optimization (SEO), PPC, Social Media, Amazon, Email, and Video Marketing. Also, with strong web design expertise in popular platforms such as Magento, Shopify, and WordPress, his company became one of the rare digital marketing agencies that provide one-stop, results-driven solutions for business clients.

Conversation with James Hsieh

Tell us about Cybertegic, the people you serve and the various types of situations that they find themselves in when they reach out to you for your help.

James Hsieh: Cybertegic started in 2002. We have a group of people who are passionate about helping small businesses grow online. Before I started this company, I used to work for Nestlé the major food supplier company worldwide. It didn't take me long to realize that if small businesses were to grow, they'd need help regarding online digital marketing. Here in Los Angeles we have a group of marketing specialist. Our sole focus is on helping small business grow online. We're Google, and Yelp certified and have talents that can help small businesses do their marketing in Google, Facebook, Amazon, or even simple email marketing.

From the perspective of a small business owner, what are the advantages being aware of online digital marketing?

James Hsieh: In today's landscape, digital marketing is evolving so quickly. New channels are coming up all the time. For example, ten years ago we had Myspace, which if you mention today, people tend to laugh about. However, we all saw the coming of age of Facebook, followed shortly thereafter by Instagram. Google advertising is currently all the rage, but before Google's era, it was Yahoo that dominated the landscape.

Regarding ecommerce product selling, Amazon came on board and dominated the market. So, the landscape is continuously changing, dynamically and rapidly. So, what we've seen is that for small business, it's tough for them not only to catch up but to keep up and understand what marketing channels are available and how to strategize and correctly use them to grow their business.

What are three of the biggest myths when it comes to effective digital marketing strategies for today's small business owners?

James Hsieh: Small business owners have a lot of concerns about digital marketing. Many of them think that digital marketing is complicated, so they're afraid to try it out. Secondly, they think digital marketing is costly, so they won't even attempt to try digital marketing. And then the third one is, some of the companies out there have had their fingers burnt by unscrupulous digital marketing companies, so they're afraid to trust digital marketing companies again. Those are some of the concerns I see for small business owners wanting to deploy digital marketing.

Could you pick one of those three examples and expand on it, please?

James Hsieh: Okay. The most common myth for small business owners is that digital marketing is too hard. The reality is it's easy to understand when you find the right team to work with. There are a lot of digital marketing companies out there, some experienced, others inexperienced. For example, students coming right out of college and staking their claim as a digital marketing company. Such companies often look great on the surface but lack real-world business experience.

I often tell small business owners that nowadays you must consider digital marketing as part of your marketing strategy.

There was a stat that I recently read that said, out of the 7.5 billion people that live on planet earth, over a 4 billion have mobile phones, with 3 billion of them on social media. So, digital marketing is here to stay, and small businesses have an advantage over big companies if they understand how to leverage social media the inexpensive way.

Recently, you may have seen that Kylie Jenner is going to be the first self-made billionaire using social media, that's a perfect example. If you understand how digital marketing works, you can leverage it to make an excellent return for your company.

Please share one or two common misconceptions about the online digital marketing.

James Hsieh: In our industry, a lot of marketing companies falsely claim what they can achieve and have achieved. So, I always advise clients, even before they hire us to please interview at least two to three other digital marketing companies. Ask to see their portfolios, and where possible, randomly pick a couple of their past clients and interview them. That way you can genuinely distinguish which digital marketing company has experience, and which don't.

For example, in terms of marketing on Google, which is something we help our clients with, there's a practice called Search Engine Optimization (SEO) that helps companies to get their website ranked in the top 10 listing of Google's first page so the site may receive free traffic and potential customers from Google.

The good thing about SEO is, the results are pretty much public information, which means if you are looking at possibly hiring a company, you can ask for proof of their accomplishments, such as the keywords they have gotten to rank. Go onto Google, search for that keyword, observe the results that come up (which should be their client). So, in other words, those obstacles can be overcome if you do a little homework. If you do so, you can easily find a reputable and experienced company to work with.

What are some of the fears that your clients have about digital marketing?

James Hsieh: Many of our clients fear the unknown. They feel that digital marketing is complicated, costly and time-consuming. But then again, going back to what I was saying before, digital marketing is vital for every company, now than ever before.

You do need the right partner to work with, so don't shortcut your company's future success by not investing the time required to search for, and interview the right companies. Once you've found one, the right company will help you to resolve your concerns, even from a budget perspective. They'll help you to navigate complex digital marketing strategies, guide you and manage your expectations, so you're adequately prepared for realistic returns on your campaigns and investments.

If business owners think that digital marketing is costly, time-consuming and complicated, what can they do get past those fears?

James Hsieh: I encourage you to look into what we call the "Four Channels of Marketing" in the US market today. You don't have to be an expert on it; you need to understand the concept behind it. There is a graphic chart on our website that helps to illustrate these four main channels of marketing.

The first significant channel is social media as in Facebook, Instagram, and YouTube channels. The second primary channel that a lot of customers use to find information is Google and Yahoo. We call this, the "Search Engine Channel." The third channel is a major one. It's "Shopping and Comparison Sites," such as Amazon and eBay, followed by the fourth and final, "Email Marketing Channel." I'm not talking about where you find email addresses to spam people, but rather once your business starts growing online, you will accumulate email addresses, which you'll want to use as a way of providing good content and promotions to bring people back to your website.

So most simply, if you understand the concept of these four channels, and work with a digital marketing company that provides detailed strategy and execution on how to grow your business, you will resolve a lot of fears and concerns you may have about implementing digital marketing campaigns.

Most digital marketing companies will conduct a free consultation session on creating a customized marketing strategy for clients. My company does that for all prospective clients because we want to make sure that they have the proper strategy before moving forward.

In your experience, what other perceived obstacles do you see that may be preventing small business owners from seeking the help of an Internet Business Consultant?

James Hsieh: As I mentioned before there are other unscrupulous digital marketing companies in the arena. For example, there was a time where a lot of Indian SEO companies promised they would generate results, guaranteed! However, the catch was, the client was told that the implementation time was about six months which is usually the minimum implementation time required for a successful SEO campaign, However, often, these unscrupulous companies would take people's money, promise the sky, and not deliver any results.

Such actions have really hurt the reputation of the digital marketing industry in general which has prevented a lot of business owners from moving forward. On the other hand, there are a lot of good digital marketing companies out there, and if you do your homework correctly and do some interviews, you will find the right company to work with. Other obstacles that hold people back from taking the next step are technical implementation and lack of resources. There are many more stumbling blocks that get in the way, but those are just a few you can overcome with the right marketing partner.

Please share an example of how you've been able to help small business owners to succeed in getting the results they want.

James Hsieh: We have a client that specializes in creating Gaming PC. It was around 2010 when he shared that he believed his industry was about takeoff. Fast forward to today, we now know just how right his prediction was because the Gaming PC industry has taken off. Despite the gaming industry's current success, back then my client was faced with the dilemma of spending too much money on Google advertisements.

After our initial consultation where we analyzed his business model, we were able to come up with strategic plans to not only help him increase the ROI on his advertisements on Google, but we deployed what we call Google (SEO), search engine optimization to help them rank on the first page of Google under its natural listing. So, what that means is that when specific keywords listed under natural listings, no matter how many times people click on that listing, it doesn't cost the client a dime.

Most importantly, more than 90% of Google users trust the information presented in the natural listing more so than the information presented in advertisements, making SEO marketing an effective method to build the authority brand image for a business online.

When we fast forward to today, my client went from a small company with a small warehouse to becoming a company that's doing hundreds of millions of dollars online per year. They have been able to reap the benefits of having a number one ranking position in Google for the keyword "Gaming PC" for the past five consecutive years.

So those are some of the achievements that we are proud to share. We're happy that we were able to help a small business to strategize, grow over time and achieve the status where they are right now.

The example I just shared is something that can be achieved by many small business owners. However, as I said before, it's important to remember that the digital marketing landscape has evolved and become even more complicated to navigate. There are the social media, Google search engine, shopping comparison sites and email channels to contend with, so I highly encourage you to do digital marketing with a professional team that can help you to navigate through the maze.

Please share one or two digital marketing pitfalls or common mistakes small business owners need to be aware of.

James Hsieh: When you're ready to deploy digital marketing to grow your business, you must be fully aware that digital marketing is a team effort between the marketing agency and your internal team. That mentality needs to be solidified among all your people.

One of the common pitfalls I come across with small business owners is they often expect that when they hire a digital marketing company, their sales will increase right away, and I need to correct that mentality.

Digital marketing companies are very good at bringing targeted traffic to any of their client's online properties, such as an Amazon account and so on, but it is the client's product pricing, promotion and business strategy that will determine whether a website visitor will want to complete a transaction. So, it will have to be a team effort where the digital marketing company will work closely with the internal sales team to generate promotions and pricing strategies, thereby enabling the business to grow over time. Not dedicating the company's internal team to work closely with the digital marketing agency can often fail the project.

Another pitfall (once traffic starts coming in), is not having a system in place for monitoring data and taking action to improve the business using the data. Data is like a gold mine. Not only for the digital marketing company, but it's essential for the business owner and his internal business team to analyze and leverage it, so they can rapidly adjust the business to market demand.

Do you have any examples of how to avoid those pitfalls in the first place, James?

James Hsieh: Regarding working together with a digital marketing company, make sure they hold a monthly meeting with you. At the very high level, the CEO and the marketing manager can quickly see some of the significant data relating to their business, which will be meaningful for both the marketing company and your small business to make the necessary changes needed to improve your business. As a small business owner, you're getting valuable insight from the market feedback on how to improve your business that is usually costly to obtain in the past. If you do this on a monthly basis, I'm pretty sure your website and business will improve over time.

You'll also want to give any digital marketing efforts, (such as advertising campaigns), at least three to six months to generate the proper results. Also, be sure to examine the results with your marketing firm on a monthly basis, rather than on a quarterly basis to ensure you are making improvements. Not giving a marketing campaign enough time to execute could result in failure to reach your desired ROI.

When you think about all those clients that you've helped to create the transformation they were looking for, what does that give you and how does that make you feel?

James Hsieh: Actually, it makes me feel really good, Stewart. I started programming when I was 15 years old. I'm a techie, and my technical career began with Nestlé, I was a Computer Systems Engineer at that time. However, during the five years I was working at Nestlé I rose quickly through the ranks and became the eBusiness Project Manager. A valuable lesson that I learned was that websites and technology alone could not generate proper returns. It is the marketing behind the technology that makes it useful and produces the appropriate returns. So, the reason I started my internet business consulting company, is that I can help to combine the technical part to the marketing part and see businesses, as I mentioned before, grow from small companies into multi-million dollar businesses. I get a great sense of satisfaction when I can help people improve their businesses over time and watch them become successful in life.

What inspired you or led you to become the Internet Business Consultant that you are today?

James Hsieh: When I was very little I sold electric fans with my father at outdoor swap meet markets. We were not a wealthy family. I was selling fans and toys to the kids in my school and trying everything to make money to help my family, so I have always had this sense of entrepreneurship and passion for creating a successful business.

I knew how hard it was to start a business and make money, so when I grew older I decided not only to get my business degree from UC Irvine, but I continued studying on and got an MBA degree from USC. I derive a firm sense of passion and happiness from being able to help people create a successful business, including myself. So, I think that's where my influence came from. My father, my family, and the focus on business is what shaped me and guided me to this path today.

Can you please share a lesson that you may have learned early on in your career that still influences how you do business today?

James Hsieh: As you may know, it's a well-known statistic that 80 percent of startups fail, while only 20 percent survive. As a consultant, I've learned how to be brutally honest with my clients (in a professional way), which helps them to avoid getting into trouble.

During my early years of consultation, I used to see a lot of people who didn't have the right idea, strategy, or resources heading into creating a business. However, even though I could see the faults in their approach, I didn't stop them from doing what's wrong. I think that is mainly because of my Asian descendants where we'd rather keep quiet than really voice our opinions to avoid confrontation. I quickly learned that even if someone has not signed a contract to become a client, I could still do them an excellent service by sharing my professional insights based on my experience in the industry.

So, by being brutally honest with people, I believe that I can help them save a lot of time, money and pain. More importantly, I can guide them into thinking in the right direction. Nowadays, if I see something that is not right, I will ask for permission to speak frankly and provide a disclaimer that this is only my opinion. Once they are clear on that, I don't hold back, whether their idea is good or not. I'm candid, speak straight from the heart and share everything I know. That has been the biggest lesson I learned very early on in my career which has helped a lot of people, and it's something I will forever stand by when consulting small business owners.

Please share three of the most critical questions that small business owners should be asking themselves while thinking about digital marketing strategies.

James Hsieh: I think the first question you should be thinking about is, how serious am I about growing my business online and am I willing to dedicate a proper advertising budget for the marketing effort?

For example, I have a small business owner who says, yes, I know digital marketing is essential, and they want to do it, but when I asked them about the time commitment and if they have allocated a budget to afford the advertisement, they couldn't come up with an answer. So, I do advise that wanting something is one thing, but committing to making it work is the essential driver that will determine if the campaign will be successful. The top 500 internet retailer businesses dedicate 10% to 12% of their annual revenue to market their business online, and as a result of that level of dedication, those businesses continue to grow rapidly.

The second question to ask yourself when looking at effective digital marketing strategies is, is your business strategy and direction clear to communicate through the marketing efforts?

Marketing can drive a lot of targeted customers to a business outline, but if your business strategy, messaging and branding are not clear, then you're not going to be able to convert visitors into loyal followers, so think through your business strategy and communications.

Lastly, ask yourself, do you have time to work with a digital marketing company closely or is there someone in your company that you can assign to work with them closely?

I'll give you an example...

We created a campaign, and we were able to drive a lot of traffic to a website, but internally we asked our client to dedicate a manager to analyze the pricing of the competition and come up with suitable competitive pricing and promotion to turn traffic into buying customers.

The truth is, very often small business owners are very busy, and they don't have the time or extra resources to assign somebody to attend to this matter. So, in a situation like that, you will end up having additional targeted traffic, but non-converting traffic. So, ask yourself and be honest about it, do you have the time or staff to work closely with a digital marketing company to make your advertising campaign successful for your company? Those are just three things of the things you should be thinking about.

What are some of the most important things that small business owners should consider when evaluating an Internet Business Consultant like yourself?

James Hsieh: Chemistry is essential when you're interviewing and talking to the company, you want to get a sense that these people have the same mentality, they're easy to work with it.

Talk to their marketing manager, or project manager, and ask them if they charge for the initial free consultation to come up with a custom marketing strategy. You'll want to work with a company that's prepared to give you the time of day to understand your business first, to come up with a marketing strategy and from there, as you go over that strategy with their team, to see if you've got the right chemistry to work together on a long-term basis. The right team working harmoniously together will help to generate the best returns for your campaigns.

What would be the best way to get in touch with you?

James Hsieh: We're very easy to find and communicate with, you can look us up online by searching on Google for our company name, Cybertegic. We have our contact phone number on the website. You can either call or email, and someone will respond right away. Once you reach out to us, you'll be in touch with our Solution Advisor who will schedule a 30-minute interview session to understand your business and business model.

Once you share some data, we will be able to research into your industry and your competition online and come up with a marketing strategy that's suitable for your business based on the advertising channels that we know are out are there.

All of this is complimentary because we believe that we need first to understand your business to see if we are the right fit to do the job. If we feel that we can, we will come up with a proposal letting you know what we can do for you. If you think that the chemistry is right, we can go from there. So again, a quick online search for our company name, 'Cybertegic' and you should see us listed on the first page of Google.

About James Hsieh
a.k.a (The Marketing Jedi)

Throughout the years of practice in digital marketing fields, James has been fortunate to be recognized by peers in the digital marketing community and has been invited to speak at various marketing conferences, trade events, radio, and even television shows.

Some of his favorite engagements are guest speaking at various television stations, radios, trade shows, businesses association conferences and at his very own annual Cybertegic Internet Business conference where he educates the public on the latest digital marketing trends that are taking place in the market today.

As a seasoned practitioner of digital marketing and a big nerd of technology by heart, James enjoys helping businesses grow through the innovative use of the latest digital marketing tactics and plans to continue to do so for many years to come.

WEBSITE
Cybertegic.com

EMAIL
James.Hsieh@Cybertegic.com

FACEBOOK
Facebook.com/CybertegicInc

LINKEDIN
LinkedIn.com/in/JamesHsieh

PHONE
+1 (626) 810-3763

LOCATION
17800 Castleton Street, Suite 638
City of Industry, CA 91748

How to Maximize Digital Marketing for Service-Based Businesses

It is the goal of every local business to drive traffic and leads to their business and with the majority of people doing an online search before engaging with a business, even local service-based businesses, it is imperative to be found at the top of the search engines if you want to compete and win in your industry.

Adam Vest, president of Denver Digital, helps companies throughout Colorado and across the country, increase their online presence by offering customized digital marketing services, including search engine optimization, website development, and social media marketing. Digital marketing can no longer be ignored by service based business and it is not a one size fits all solution either. Vest explains the holistic approach to a good digital marketing campaign that gets results.

Conversation with Adam Vest

Tell us a little bit more about yourself, Adam and how Denver Digital came about.

Adam Vest: About three years ago I was working for a national advertising agency as an account executive, basically selling pay per click and directory placement. And at that time the company that I was working for did not offer SEO services. So, I would be running these appointments with my clients and you know, nine times out of 10 they would end up asking me how to rank their website organically on the major search engines.

And you know, I realized early on that I wasn't necessarily in a position to be able to help my customers. And, that was very frustrating for me because as you know, pay per click leads can get pretty costly and search engine optimization, generally speaking, is a much lower cost per lead. It was also difficult not having control over the products that I was selling because I wasn't the one running the campaign. At the end of the day, that's what led me to start Denver Digital.

Is SEO the large part of your business or is that more web design?

Adam Vest: Yes. So, search engine optimization is kind of the core of what we do. However, website design and development certainly tie into that significantly.

What kind of clients is it that you help? Is there any niche that you like to stick with?

Adam Vest: Well, we focus heavily on the service industry. We have clients that range from national hat companies to roofing companies to HVAC companies to eCommerce, a bow tie guy; so, we kind of run the gambit as far as the clients that we're able to help and that we're interested in partnering with.

What kind of problems are those types of service industries having?

Adam Vest: I would say the majority of service industry businesses that have been around for a while have certainly done SEO or pay per click or direct mail. But, as far as some of the biggest challenges that I see is really just a lack of online presence. I think most business owners at this point have figured out how to set up their Google My Business page and have a pretty good understanding of how to build or promote Facebook ads or posts, but I think one of the biggest challenges is really knowing how to accurately define their target market as well as their customers and that's going to end up turning a click into an actual phone call or a sale.

Is all traffic created equal?

Adam Vest: If I could bring you 500 visitors to your site and not one of them made the call, versus if we were to bring you one visitor that ended up turning into a customer, which one would be more powerful? Obviously the one that would turn into an actual sale.

What kinds of things do you do to really target the right audience?

Adam Vest: Well, I think the foundation of any good SEO campaign is the actual website. I hear a lot of people say, when they're talking about the foundations of a campaign, I hear a lot of keyword analysis, things like that. But without a website, your keyword analysis doesn't really matter. So, I think having an easy to read, easy to navigate website, well coded, not having a lot of bloat within the code of the site is really important and it's a great starting point. The work really begins once we have developed a great website for a customer.

What affects the speed of a website?

Adam Vest: One of the biggest factors I think that affects the speed of a website is having all that extra bloatware in the form of different plugins. So, I think a lot of folks will end up installing additional code into the site and then they just kind of forget it. They might not be using it and it's just kind of staying on the site taking up space and really slowing down the site. We always try and target a three second or lower load time for websites just because once you start getting into the four, five and six second range, you have a significant drop off from customers just backing out of the site or going into to the next site that will load a little bit faster.

From a technical aspect, what kind of things can you do to make the site load faster?

Adam Vest: There are a whole lot of things and I don't want to get too technical. But, making sure that a) you don't have any unnecessary plugins b) that you are caching the site and that the site is set up correctly. You don't have extra CSS all throughout the site that's slowing things down. That's another big issue that we see would be CSS that's not coded correctly. So those are two of the biggest things. And then, of course, I think most importantly it's just tracking to figure out exactly what your load speed is, and then finding the right ways, whether it's images, images can take up a lot of space on the site. So, a downsizing or resizing of those images can make a large impact as well.

What other things are you seeing that are important if you are in an industry where the competition is tough?

Adam Vest: Something that's really become very prevalent over the past few years would be the map pack. So, the top three sections in the maps, especially for our service industry clients. A lot of times folks will Google something and they'll see on their phone, they'll do a mobile search, they'll see one of the three businesses there in the map section and they'll just directly call. We've seen tremendous success by focusing on the map pack for all our customers.

How do we get in the map pack?

Adam Vest: That's a great question and it's a question that I hear just about every day. So, from what we've found, there are three main factors when it comes to getting into that map pack. First and foremost is having high-quality backlinks leading to your site. Secondly, would be the number of reviews that you have. And then, of course, the location that you're searching from. So, those are the three biggest factors. Google My Business now has come a long way, and really optimizing your Google My Business page is more important now than ever before.

What does optimizing the GMB page mean?

Adam Vest: Well, first and foremost, you have to have the correct categories. You have to have the right phone number, a number consistent online throughout all of the different directories. You have to have the right citations; some other things that can really play a factor would be sharing blog posts on your Google My Business page. It's not something that I see that's done often and I think it's a big missed opportunity. Sharing blog posts, sharing updates, you can now create events. There's a lot of things that you can do to really utilize the Google My Business page and obviously, Google loves that kind of stuff. They tend to give preferential treatment to the businesses that are doing that.

Where do you think things are going with the map rankings?

Adam Vest: Well, I think just recently Google started offering advertising in the map pack and I can't imagine that that's not making them money. So, at the end of the day, you really have to think about if you're looking at where it's all headed, you really need to think about what's going to be best for Google. And I think advertising in the map pack is very important. I think that there's a challenge right now to figure out how to incorporate the map pack into a voice search. So, when a consumer is searching with their Alexa, what are the top roofing companies in my area? I think what we're seeing right now is Google is trying very hard to figure out how to dish out that information. And I think it's going to come down to reviews. I think the more reviews, the more five star four and five-star reviews that you can get the better. I think it's more important now than ever before.

Talk to me about the actual placing of the maps on the search engine result page versus the organic results which seem to get pushed further and further down, especially for these services businesses.

Adam Vest: Sure. And I think at some point the organic results might end up on page two with the way things are going, as far as the AdWords that Google shows on the search engine results page. But, map section shows directly below the Google ads. So, you have three Google ads below that you're going to have the map pack, the three pack, and then below that, you're going to end up having the organic section. Now, as I mentioned earlier, in some industries there are now four different maps business showing up in that map pack, one of them being an advertisement.

Another thing that's popped up recently for service-based industries are these Google sponsored ads as well, which show up above or below the regular ads.

Adam Vest: That's exactly right. I believe it's called the Google guarantee. It can be very powerful for companies that go through the process. It's a pretty stringent process to become a Google verified business with that guarantee. But, it certainly is a conversation that I've had with all my accounts because it did just recently happen. I think they were Beta testing it on the west coast there for years and then just recently rolled out to quite a few major cities.

How important are the actual quality of links and the content on the website to actually rank on the map?

Adam Vest: I think those are two of the most important things that you can do for search engine optimization, other than having clean code on the website, would be having fantastic content that's not built for the search engines, but that's built for consumption. And then, on the same token, having high-quality backlinks is one of the most important factors in determining your ranking. So, there can be a client with a backlink profile of over a thousand backlinks or 50,000 backlinks and then you can have a client with a handful of backlinks that are very high quality and that handful of backlinks will get that client to rank higher than having thousands and thousands of junk backlinks, broken links, things like that.

What exactly does a high-quality backlink look like?

Adam Vest: Well, what we like to say, domain authority is not necessarily a term that Google uses, but I think everybody in the industry kind of knows that they still look at page rank. They still look at DA. We kind of have a cut off when it comes to who we will backlink to. So, your site needs to have authority for us to link our clients to your site. And I think at the end of the day, a lot of those relationships are developed over time. So, having the right relationships with website owners, with business owners all around the country and especially here locally is very important because there are a lot of websites that have a very low domain authority score. You know, if you're looking at Moz or, or one of these tools that still does show the DA Score, we have a threshold that we're not going to go under as far as linking to their site.

If you get a link from a good quality trusted site with a high domain authority and it's relevant to your business, is there any backend SEO you could do pointing to that link?

Adam Vest: Well, you can certainly link out to whoever was kind enough to link to you in the first place. What we've found generally what's generating these high-quality backlinks is great content and I think focusing on the content is extremely important in 2018. That was not always the case, but, the crawlers over at Google are getting smarter and smarter by the minute and they understand great content versus average content versus bad content. I think at this point having a great content development team is critical to the success of any agency and the success of any business owner as well.

How is mobile having an effect on local results?

Adam Vest: Mobile has revolutionized the industry. If you remember back to the days you know, not that long ago, we didn't have cell phones. So now, we have these little computers in our pocket that can pretty much do anything that we need them to do as far as finding information. So, we're seeing the majority of the searches come in on mobile devices, whether that's an iPad or a tablet or a cell phone, whatever the case and optimizing for mobile now is an absolute necessity. Google gives you a significant ding if your site is not mobile optimized. You can still have a website that's mobile optimized and still not going to convert. So, it's important to pay attention to both the desktop and the mobile versions of your site if you really want to achieve the goals that you've set out to achieve with your online presence.

What's the first thing that you do to explain all these things to new clients?

Adam Vest: Initially we'll sit down with a client, and all the packages that we offer are tailor-made to each individual client. So, I think listening is really one of the most important things that we can do to start the relationship off on the right foot. And it really also helps to build trust when a client or a customer knows that they're not just another number within your agency, but you actually take the time to get to know their business. That's very powerful. So, initially, we'll spend a significant amount of time doing keyword research for each client. But over time, we've been around for over three years now, so we're starting to kind of see the same keywords over and over again for different industries. However, there's what's called long tail keywords which are becoming more and more prevalent. So, because of that voice capability, the voice search capability, long tail keywords are important to optimize for as well. It's going more and more in that direction. There's just no getting around it when you have voice connected devices all around you, Siri, Alexa, Google, it's extremely important to optimize your site for those long tail keywords that are going to get you found with some of these mobile devices.

How do you find these long tail keywords and what kind of content do you have to generate to make them rank?

Adam Vest: Well, as you said, it's generating content and the way that we specifically find these long tail keywords is based on the industry. We'll come up with 50 keywords that we're targeting, and we'll track those 50 keywords. A lot of agencies will track three, five, 10 keywords at a time. We like to track at least 50. The more, the better as far as we're concerned. And what we do is based on the volume, based on our different analytics tools, we're able to kind of see exactly how many searches are being done. It always surprises me to see some of these long tail keywords that people are using their voice to search for. But, optimizing for them is critical these days and one of the ways that we'll go about finding them and I think a lot of people miss this is to just start to search Google for that industry in the form of a question and what will end up happening is you'll see a list of quite a few of the most common long tail keywords that you have to choose from.

Could you give me an example of that?

Adam Vest: So, if you're looking for "best roofers in Denver", or if you're looking for who is the "best garage door repair company near me", what you're going to end up seeing is about 5 to 10 variations of that actual search. And that would be considered a long tail keyword. And you just come up with 10 to 15 of these searches. You start typing them into Google and you're going to see a significant amount by the time you're done, you're going to have 40, 50, 60 different long tail keywords that you want to rank for.

When you have a list of your long tail keywords, do you have to write a page for each one of them or do you try and include many of the keywords in one longer blog post or article?

Adam Vest: We'll target around two long tail keywords per piece of content that we write, whether that's an actual webpage or if it's a blog. Then, of course, you want to link from that anchor text using that specific long tail keyword. If you can link to other places within your site, what that's doing is it's telling Google what the page is about. Then also there are things like Schema markup to where you can be the expert, the authority when answering these questions. You know, if you type in a question to Google, you'll see that little snippet and as long as you're optimizing properly the goal is to be able to be the authoritative resource for Google to use and they'll actually put your information right there and then of course they link to your website as well. So, it's a very powerful tool.

What are some of the misconceptions that you hear about SEO?

Adam Vest: How much time do we have left Neil? There's quite a few. I think I could probably talk about this for the entire half hour here. It varies customer to customer and industry to industry. But from what I've seen, some of the biggest misconceptions surround pricing. A lot of business owners think that search engine optimization costs thousands and thousands and thousands of dollars a month, which is not always the case. Some other things that we hear all the time are, it just doesn't work. We don't get leads from our website. My answer to that usually is, how are people finding you if you're not showing up in front of the customers who are actively searching for you? How would you ever get leads on your website? So, that's a big misconception, we've never gotten leads in the past. Why would that change now? And then also a lot of the technical aspects of SEO kind of can put some business owners off.

What holds people back from actually taking the initiative in talking to an SEO like yourself?

Adam Vest: I think it's just kind of a fear of what they might not necessarily understand or what they're familiar with. I don't think anybody wants to spend money on something that they're not going to get any kind of return from. And I think that's the biggest fear for most clients is what happens if I spend this money and nothing happens.

What are the expectations for starting an SEO campaign?

Adam Vest: First and foremost, if anyone tells you that they can guarantee a ranking, you know, we all get these emails 100 times a day, even myself being the president of an advertising agency, I get these emails from overseas saying, "Rank first page, first position within 90 days." So, anybody that tells you a specific timeframe, an exact time frame is not being completely forthcoming with you. But on average, what we see is dependent on the industry and depending on whether it's local or not, if it's a national search, this would be different...but, locally three to six months, as long as we're doing things the right way, as long as we're building high-quality links, as long as we're writing great content, generally speaking, we'll see accounts start to rank within three to six months.

It also is very dependent on your website. So, if we start from scratch, if we build the site for you, it's going to take longer because your site does not have that authority, that domain authority or that time online. My favorite accounts to work with are the accounts that are primed and ready to go. The accounts that have been online for 10 years, they have all of these natural links that have been built without necessarily a lot of these business owners even realizing it and they just haven't made any tweaks. They haven't made any adjustments on their site because it was working 10 years ago and they didn't want to change things. So those are the accounts that we can generally get to rank relatively quickly.

What kind of results should a local service based company expect when they implement an SEO program?

Adam Vest: I'll give you an example of a client that I just spoke with yesterday. So, we started working together two years ago, he's a garage door repair guy here in Colorado Springs, so down south and during our meeting he had told me in the prime of his career he was doing about 100 new garage door replacements per month and unfortunately, he was down to about 10 replacement doors per month when him and I first met. He had a lot of similar questions as far as what you're asking and he trusted in the process. Over the past 30 days, he's seen just from the map pack over 110 phone calls just from the map pack alone.

Wow! That's tremendous!

Adam Vest: Yes, he's thrilled about it and it's always a good conversation anytime that I'm able to speak with him.

Do you have any other success stories that really stick out in your mind?

Adam Vest: We've worked with roofers that show up if you Google 'Denver roofers' or 'roofers Denver' or 'roofing company Denver'. Our guys show up in the top position. Nationally, we worked with a hat company that we were able to take from page seven to page one, position one for the search 'fitted hats'. That generated a lot of traffic for them. We just recently finished up a campaign with a bow tie company that has a significant e-commerce site and we were able to get him to rank number one nationally for the search 'bow tie'. And it was great to see because right below him was Macy's.

So, some big players in the industry, we were able to allow him to compete with those, with those larger companies.

If somebody is looking for an SEO company to do work for them, Adam, what kind of questions should they be asking to make sure that they are talking to the right company?

Adam Vest: I think some of the most important questions would be, how long have you been in the industry doing search engine optimization? Secondly, what type of backlinks are you going to be sending to the website? Because, as I mentioned earlier, sending the wrong type of backlinks can really have a negative effect on your placement online. Finally, I would ask for examples. I would ask for examples and have them show you right then and there. Say, "Show me someone that you've gotten to the front page or the front position in a competitive industry". I think results speak for themselves and it's something that we take great pride in are the results that we've been able to achieve for our clients. It's a very important question to ask but often gets overlooked.

If somebody wants to reach out to you and get help for their SEO campaign what's the best way for them to do that?

Adam Vest: Visit MyDenverDigital.com or we just recently launched a large city guide here in Denver, which is DenverDigital.com.

Or you can email me Adam@DenverDigital.com, or give us a call. 720-316-4217

Briefly talk to me about the DenverDigital.com. What exactly is that?

Adam Vest: Our goal is to create the largest city guide here in Denver. So, it's an online business directory and lifestyle website. It's also a place for folks to find out what's going on in the city and throughout Colorado in general. There are job offerings, events, hotel and restaurant bookings, sports schedules, local breweries and more. There are a lot of benefits I think for both business owners and consumers. Denver is a unique market. I think last year we had over 70,000 new residents come to Denver, so we wanted to provide something that was going to kind of showcase this wonderful city.

About Adam Vest

Adam Vest is the President of Denver Digital and a digital marketing strategist with more than eight years of experience in helping businesses form creative, customized online marketing strategies that are centered around search engine optimization (SEO) best practices. Since the start of his career, Vest has become a leader in the online advertising industry.

His accomplishments are vast. In the past decade, Vest has built multiple successful companies and has helped hundreds of business owners across the country achieve success online.

Vest's current clients include both national retailers along with local, mom-and-pop service companies. His goal is to provide effective, customer online marketing campaigns "that allow the little guy to compete with the big guy."

PHONE
720-316-4217

EMAIL
Adam@denverdigital.com

WEBSITE
MyDenverDigital.com
DenverDigital.com

LINKEDIN
LinkedIn.com/in/AdamVestDenverColorado

What to do if You Get Pulled Over for DUI

Jim Yeargan is a **DUI attorney in Atlanta** with *Yeargan and Kert, LLC*. He helps business owners, executives, and other licensed professionals stop criminal charges from destroying their lives. DUI is a serious offence that carries severe life altering penalties if convicted. His clients fear their lives will spiral out of control if they get a DUI conviction on their record. A DUI attorney for 15 years, Mr. Yeargan has put prior experience as a DUI prosecutor in Atlanta to work for his clients. Prior to working for the defense, he not only prosecuted DUI cases, but he also trained prosecutors in DUI cases, and he taught at police academies. Now he uses that knowledge and experience to his clients' advantage.

Conversation with Jim Yeargan

Give us a little bit about your background, and how you became a DUI lawyer, and how long Yeargan and Kert has been in business.

Jim Yeargan: I've been a DUI attorney for 15 years. And this isn't what I first thought I'd go into, but I'm thankful that I found it. It's a very interesting field, and you get to work with a lot of great people, and help them out, and stop these things from ruining and devastating their lives. I began my career as a DUI prosecutor and did that for three years in the city of Atlanta. And that's really where I cut my teeth and learned everything. And it was a great opportunity, because I got to work with the police and the taskforce officers. I got to know all the prosecutors and the judges. And then after I'd been there for a while, I was able to start training people. So, I'd train the prosecutors, and I would go to the police academy and teach them how to testify in court, and write police reports, and things like that. So, I had a very strong foundation on that side.

And then when I was able to start doing defense work, I was able to use all of that, of course, to my advantage and my clients' advantage. So, it was a really great way to start my career.

What kind of clients is it that you tend to help?

Jim Yeargan: I really enjoy working with people who... Of course, everyone wants to beat their charges... but who basically have, I hate to phrase it this way, but something to lose. It's nice working with professionals, doctors, lawyers, accountants, pilots, people like that, who really care about the outcome of their case and really don't want their lives disrupted by it. You know mainly, when people first get this charge, they kind of go into a downward spiral of thinking that their life is over, and it's going to cost them their career, their family, their driver's license, their ability to earn a living, everything. And it's nice to be able to help them out of that spiral and show them that that's not going to happen.

Some people, they amaze me, some people get a DUI, and not just DUIs, but criminal charges in general, and they just don't care. They're like, "Oh, I'll just go plead guilty to it," or you know, they have a long record, it doesn't matter to them. But I enjoy working with people who don't want this to interrupt their lives, or disrupt their lives, and want to get everything back on track, and get this behind them. So basically, when I say people with something to lose, they're wanting to keep their life as it is, keep their family intact, keep their job, their ability to work, all of that.

So, talk to me about some of those consequences if there is a DUI on record. What does that mean to a professional?

Jim Yeargan: It really varies by profession, and that's why when you're looking for a DUI lawyer, you need someone who knows the ins and outs, because many times, you're dealing with more than just the actual criminal charges. You're dealing with what's going to happen to the job, the driver's license, insurance rates, things like that. But for instance, if a pilot gets a DUI and they're convicted, they'll never fly again. They're grounded for life. So, when you have those cases, you definitely need to be very careful. And they need to hire someone who knows what they're doing. Lawyers, it used not to be such a big deal, but especially the State Bar of Georgia, they take more of an interest now if an attorney gets a DUI, because they're worried about attorneys going into downward spirals or using alcohol as a crutch. And they don't want that to impact their practice.

Nursing, many times nurses will have to jump through many hoops, go through appeal processes to have their nursing licenses renewed, because the board is afraid that with alcohol, there might be a drug problem. Nurses have, you know, many nurses have unfettered access to drugs. So, a lot of times, you'll have to go through the appeal process with them to make, to let the board understand that it was just DUI alcohol, there's not a drug problem there, and that they can still be around medications. So, it really varies on each, how the person's employed, basically.

What is the state of mind when somebody first gives you a call? What's on their mind? What questions, what concerns do they have? And how are you able to help ease some of those concerns right away?

Jim Yeargan: They're usually in a pretty bad place. They're usually depressed, sad, scared. A lot of times, they're beating themselves up. And many times, people aren't aware that their blood alcohol concentration was as high as it is or was, so they're very disappointed, because they really didn't think they were doing something wrong. And then they have all this evidence and alleged proof that something else has happened. So many times, they're worried about their driver's license. They think they're going to lose it for a year and not be able to drive. So, they're worried about getting to and from work, especially if they work in outside sales, or if they're in any type of pharmaceutical sales; or their job has company insurance, or they drive a company car. They're worried about getting their kids to school and to other activities. They're worried about going to the grocery store.

So, it really impacts, not just the career, but daily life as well. All of that comes in on them, and they're really worried about, basically, how they're going to do their daily activities and function.

Talk to me about the blood alcohol level. What is the allowable level? How many drinks? Is there a safe amount of alcohol to be drinking before driving?

Jim Yeargan: In Georgia, the legal limit is .08. And what that means is, if they have a test on you ... This is, of course, what the prosecutor's saying ... that at .08 or higher, whether you're feeling it or not, you're legally drunk. Of course, you know, some people who drink a lot, they can be a .08, a .10, some could be double, even triple that, and not feel the effects because they drink a lot. Georgia also has what's called their "less safe" statute, so say your blood alcohol concentration is not a .08, say it's below that. Say you get pulled over, arrested for a DUI, and you're a .06. Well, they still charge you with what's called "less safe."

So, in this case, they're trying to say that while you weren't .08 or higher, they feel that the alcohol was affecting your ability to drive, to the point that you're a less safe driver. So even though you blew under the legal limit, they're still going to charge you with a DUI, and that's where the numbers come into play. Now of course, the .08 or higher, that's for drivers, age 21 or older and drivers who are not commercial drivers or CDLs. For the average person on the street driving a car, .08 or higher is the limit.

Is that one drink, two drinks?

Jim Yeargan: Again, that varies quite a bit from person to person. You know, bigger guys, they can drink more. Women, you know, sometimes one drink will do it. That's what we hear a lot, especially in females, is they'll go out to dinner, and they'll just have a glass of wine, maybe two. And they're smaller, and their blood alcohol concentration will be a .10 or a .12. It really depends on the person, what they've had to eat that day, things like that. That's why it's really a wildcard.

A lot of people think, incorrectly, but they think that zero tolerance is the law, where if you have any amount of alcohol in your system, you're not allowed to drive, legally. And that's not true in Georgia. In Georgia, you can drink and drive as long as you're not .08 or above, or you're less safe. Sometimes people get will pulled over, and they'll say, "Oh, I told the officer I had two or three drinks. I shouldn't have done that." Well, that's fine, because again, you can drink and drive. You just can't be over the limit or "less safe." You know, I tell people, in this day and age, don't drink and drive. It's just not worth it, because when they pull you over, and they smell the alcohol coming off you, whether you've had a drink or two, it's probably all downhill from there.

The other problem with that is prescription medication, because a lot of times, officers will pull people over, and their blood alcohol concentration will be fairly low. It might even be .04, .03. And then the next question is, "Well, which medicines do you take?" And if you tell them, you know, you take antidepressants, or you take any type of pain medicine, or blood pressure medicine, whether you've taken it for 10 or 15 years, then they're going to say, "Well, now you're DUI,

EXPERT PROFILES · 57

combination alcohol and medication," saying that the two are working together to affect your driving.

What is the sentence for somebody that has been drinking and driving and is over the limit?

Jim Yeargan: For a first offense in Georgia, we have different look back periods. The first look back period, as far as your license is concerned, is a five-year look back. You want to see if the person has any other DUI convictions in a five-year period. And that five-year period is measured from date of arrest to date of arrest. It's not when the case closes. In some of the jurisdictions in Georgia, it can take two or three years for a case to close, so that's why they use the arrest date. That's as far as license sanctions.

If you only have one DUI conviction in a five-year period ... And this is not taking into account administrative license suspensions, because there are many different suspensions you can deal with. But as far as the actual conviction, it's 120-day license suspension. And there's a limited permit for work, school, doctor's appointments, things of that nature. As far as the actual court punishment goes, you're generally looking at 40 hours of community service, a fine of anywhere from $300 to $1,000. Again, that varies from court to court. Roughly, you're looking at, most jurisdictions, $300, maybe a $700 fine. They add surcharges on. You're not being punished for going to court. Those are just state fines and fees you pay. Even if you pay a speeding ticket, you pay those. But on a DUI, they're so high they can actually double the fine.

So, on a $500 fine, you usually end up paying a total of about $1,000. You have to go to DUI school, which takes a weekend. You usually have to do a drug and alcohol evaluation, which takes about an hour. And then you have to do 12 months of probation. And most judges will let that probation become non-reporting once you complete everything, which means you don't have to check in with them once a month; but other judges won't. You may have to make a trip once a month to the probation officer, just to check in, so they can take a look at you. They may drug test you. Usually, you have to pay about $49 a month while you're reporting to the probation, so that's an extra expense.

The next look back period is a 10-year look back period. And this is different from the suspensions, but if you have more than one DUI in Georgia within a 10-year period, the fines and penalties really increase. The fines go up several hundred dollars, but the community service goes up from 40 hours to 240 hours. There's a minimum requirement of three days in jail, and that's if you can get the minimum. Some judges like to give 10, some even like to give 30 days in jail. And then you still have to do the DUI school, drug and alcohol evaluation. A lot of judges will make you do a MADD Victim Impact Panel, which is a two-hour lecture put on by Mothers Against Drunk Driving, you go to one time. Some judges require AA, depending on how many DUIs you have in that 10-year period.

And then, of course, if you have more than one DUI in the five-year period, if you're really cramming them in there, you start getting into ignition interlock devices put on your car. That's the device you have to blow into before your vehicle will start. So, when people start getting them within the 5- and 10-year look back period, the punishments skyrocket. They build up exponentially. And then the final look back period is over a lifetime. So, if you had a DUI 20 years ago, the prosecutor, the judge can still take that into account. Now, that's not as serious. There are no, basically, mandatory minimums on lifetime look backs. Once you're outside of that 10-year period, there's not a minimum sentence that the court has to give you, such as the three days in jail and the 240 hours of community service. Older DUIs, they usually don't up the punishment, but some jurisdictions do. Some judges will. You have to be careful, even if you have a DUI that's 15, 25 years old.

What can you do to prevent some of these things going on the record?

Jim Yeargan: It's a case-by-case basis. Sometimes, we get the charges totally dismissed. We've done that many, many times, where even the moving violation gets thrown out. And I say even the moving violation because usually, when you take these cases to trial, you may beat the DUI charge, but the individual is usually convicted of speeding or failure to maintain lane, which is on the video. You know, those are usually hard to beat because the proof is right there. It did happen. But many times, we have been able to get the whole case dismissed. Sometimes, we're able to get the DUI reduced to a lesser charge; usually reckless driving, which sounds worse than it is, but in Georgia, that's just like a fast speeding ticket. It's just a regular moving violation.

And in those cases, you still pay a fine, and do community service, go to DUI school. You basically get a DUI sentence. But the trade-off is, you don't get your license suspended. You don't get the DUI on your driving history. And the big part is, you can tell future employers or your current employer that you are not convicted of a DUI. And in some instances, we can even get it lower than reckless driving, just get it to the moving violation; sometimes, you know, running a stop sign or speeding. So, it really depends on a case-by-case basis, but if we can't get the case totally dismissed, we do always try to get it reduced.

Is there anything that someone who has been pulled over can say or prevent from saying that's going to help their case?

Jim Yeargan: I tell everyone that they have to make this decision for themselves when it happens. But then I say, if I were in the position where I'd been drinking, and I get pulled over, I would refuse the field sobriety test. They're voluntary. They can't force you to follow their finger with your eyes, or to walk the line, or to stand on one leg. I would not take any breath, blood, or any chemical test. Just refuse them. Don't admit to drinking. Be polite. Just say, "Yes, sir. No, sir. Yes, ma'am. No, ma'am." Don't talk too much. Just answer their questions shortly. And again, if they ask, you know, "Why don't you want to do these tests," you can say, "Well, I met a lawyer once, and he said it's best not to do this."

But keep in mind, when you refuse to do everything, you are going to get arrested. They're not going to throw their hands up and say, "Oh, well you're free to go." But if you have been drinking, if you are intoxicated, and you don't do the tests, you're putting yourself in a better position to fight the charge; because they're not going to have a whole lot of evidence to hold against you.

If you are arrested, are the police able to do the tests once they get you to the jail?

Jim Yeargan: In Georgia, they request that you take the tests. Now if you refuse, what they can do is, they can go to a judge, and everything's computerized now, so it's not like it used to be. They can get a warrant and do what's called a forced blood draw. And they will take you to the hospital. And you know, if you fight them, you'll actually be held down, and they'll put a taser to you and say, "If you kick, we're going to shock you," and have a nurse draw your blood.

Now, most jurisdictions don't do that anymore. Some do, and some officers, any officer can go get this warrant. But they generally don't, because by the time it takes them to contact the judge, do all the computer work, get the warrant, take you to the hospital, draw the blood, then take you to the jail, they could have been on the road and probably arrested three or four other people in that timeframe.

Some officers will do that, but the majority are not going to actually go get a warrant and take your blood. It is a possibility that they could force you, but they don't do it the way they used to. That was very popular a couple of years ago. More officers were doing it. But most do not.

What other fears go through their mind when they are first pulled over?

Jim Yeargan: Many times, they just, they equate it to a speeding ticket, because that's probably ... or a traffic ticket. That's probably the encounter most people have with the police. So, they think, "Well, if I'm cooperative and I do everything the officer says, he's going to let me go." So that's why a lot of people decide to do the field test. They decide to blow. You know, they basically go along to get along. And in a DUI case, it's not like a speeding ticket, where they may issue you a warning or just charge you with a few miles over the limit. They're not going to let you go once they smell the alcohol. So a lot of times, people have the misconception that if they're very friendly, the officer will just release them. Now, it's always good to be friendly. You know, there's no need to be rude or fight. And again, be respectful. But that's why I tell people to refuse everything, because they're not going to let you go. You're just going to dig your hole deeper by trying to cooperate and agree with them.

Give me an example of a situation that you've come across where you were able to really help somebody out. And what did it mean to them?

Jim Yeargan: Recently, we had a pilot. We were able to get all of his charges reduced. And that meant he could keep his job. And pilots, those are great jobs, and they get paid a lot of money. Had he been convicted, he literally would have lost his ability to work, because they pull your pilot's license. We've helped, recently, another person who was going through a child custody dispute. His wife was trying to use the arrest and everything against him, even though his kids were not in the car. It didn't have anything to do, directly, with that situation. But of course, her attorney was trying to say, "Oh, he's been arrested. He has a drug problem, an alcohol problem." We were able to get all of that dismissed, so that wasn't able to be used against him. So, it's really interesting how DUI affects so many different areas of a person's life, depending on what's going on at that particular moment.

Divorce is still very common. If there is a DUI on somebody's record, what does that mean as far as the custody of children?

Jim Yeargan: Absolutely. That, again, the other side can use that against them and try to say that, you know, they're not fit to be around children, or they're not a good parent. Even if it's just the first arrest, they worry that this is going to develop into a pattern and keep occurring. Divorces are already contentious enough. Adding an arrest and now a criminal record into that doesn't help. A lot of jurisdictions also post your mugshots online. When people call, they're worried about, "Oh, I'm going through a divorce. Is my soon to be ex-wife going to be able to find this?" And even if they're not going through a divorce, or you know, "Will my employer see my mugshot online? If someone Googles my name, is this going to come up," things like that.

In this society, where we have so much technology, that's a huge downfall, placing those mugshots online.

You mentioned earlier that you're a specialist in DUI cases. Can any type of lawyer defend a DUI case?

Jim Yeargan: Unfortunately, any type of lawyer can, and a lot of lawyers will take a DUI case. To be honest, there's a lot of money in it. Many of these guys will charge a lot of money and not do anything for you. DUI has actually been declared, by the American Bar Association, to be a subspecialty. So that's why when you hire a DUI lawyer, you need to ask, you know, not only about their experience, but if they have certain certifications, like if they're certified in field sobriety testing. Are they certified as a student, or are they certified as an instructor? Have they taken the classes and are certified on the breath testing machines? Have they taken the drug recognition evaluator classes? Have they taken other drugs that impair driving classes, things like that? There are many, many classes and certifications that real DUI lawyers, people that actually do this all the time, have; that lawyers who are just trying to get money and flip the cases with pleas will not have.

What does that look like for the client? How much does a DUI case tend to cost?

Jim Yeargan: It varies quite a bit from lawyer to lawyer. But for good, solid representation, it's going to run you anywhere from a starting point of $5,000, depending on your record and other factors, up to $10,000 or $15,000.

What holds people back from not getting the right help?

Jim Yeargan: I think it's they don't understand. They will talk to a bunch of lawyers, and they'll get the $5,000 or $10,000 quotes. Then they'll talk to other lawyers and get the $1,500, or the $2,000 quote, or even lower. And I don't think they really understand what all goes into fighting one of these cases. In Georgia, a DUI case is actually the hardest case to try because of the science, the ever-changing law. There's so much involved in it. It's not just something you can pick up and do. So, I don't think they really understand that specialized lawyers are needed in this case.

Also, people ask for recommendations. And they get lots of recommendations from this friend, or this person knows someone who helped someone else. And of course, they don't know who that person is, or what their case was, or what the lawyer did. But it's not like a credential. So, they go and talk to this person, and they just don't realize that the lawyer they're talking to is not in the best position to help them with their particular set of facts.

What is it about this industry that you really liked? Why do you continue to be in this area of defense?

Jim Yeargan: It's really a fascinating area, but the main thing is, I get to work with so many interesting people, and just really good people from all different walks of life. You know, you do some areas of criminal defense, and honestly, you're just dealing with people who just aren't good people. But with DUIs, it's professionals, and people who just made a mistake, or didn't realize maybe they had one too many. And in some cases, they're going to pick someone else up who was too drunk to drive, so they think they're doing the right thing. So, you get to work with really good people who just made not the best decision one night. And they're very scared, and you get to help them put their lives back together and get back on track.

What is the best way for people to contact you if they want your help to represent them?

Jim Yeargan: They can contact us through our website, which is AtlantaDuiLawyer.com; or directly on the phone number, which is 404-467-1747. Or they can email me directly at Jim@DuiJim.com.

About Jim Yeargan

James Yeargan is one of the most respected, and sought after Atlanta DUI Lawyers. His successful defense record, and unprecedented devotion to his clients, has earned him this honor. Mr. Yeargan's reputation as a tenacious DUI practitioner, coupled with his remarkable trial strategy and indomitable presence in the courtroom, have earned him the moniker "DUI Jim" throughout the Atlanta community, and Georgia at large. It is his dedication to his clients that makes Mr. Yeargan 's DUI practice so unique and sought after.

WEBSITE
AtlantaDUILawyer.com

EMAIL
Jim@DUIJim.com

PHONE
(404) 467 1747

How to Attract More Leads for Doctors, Attorneys and Dentists

Every business needs a steady stream of traffic and leads and the internet is the place where those prospects go to search for business reputation and reviews prior to making a decision. Knowing how to be found and communicate with these ideal prospects is vital in today's competitive marketplace. Doctors, Attorneys, and Dentists who utilize this platform to share their authority and credibility have an unfair advantage over those who rely on word of mouth and referrals alone.

Dan is the president and owner of Page 1 Solutions LLC, which is an Internet Marketing company specializing in website development and digital marketing for attorneys, doctors and dentists. In addition to website design and development, Page 1, handles the SEO and pay per click campaigns for clients as well as designing and managing social media and display advertising campaigns. At Page 1, Dan writes content and produces videos for his clients and has written numerous articles and given many presentations on internet marketing for professionals. Dan shares what is working for doctors, dentists and attorneys in this interview.

Conversation with Dan Goldstein

What kind of issues do doctors, dentists, and attorneys have and why do they come to you?

Dan Goldstein: There are a lot of similarities between what our clients deal with and what other businesses deal with, in terms of their internet marketing. One big difference, in the case of our clients, they are all marketing specific services, as opposed to products. An attorney, a plastic surgeon or an ophthalmologist are providing services to their customers as opposed to other businesses that are selling specific products. It's a little bit different when you are marketing a service versus marketing a product. Some of the same issues are likely present in both.

What are the different issues then when it comes to marketing a service? How do you market specifically for that service?

Dan Goldstein: We work with clients throughout the country and in Canada. We have a few other clients outside of those two areas, but almost all our clientele is throughout North America. In terms of what's different, it's really important to engage and make a connection with their prospective customer, whereas in the case of a product, you know, fill in the blank. For example, if you are selling a soccer ball, you can buy that soccer ball online. You can look at reviews and you can place your order online and have it shipped to you and it arrives in a few days. In the case of a service, the business actually needs to find a way to connect with a potential customer over the phone or in person so they can have the opportunity to form a connection that encourages the customer to choose that practice. So, the key thing that we try to do is create enough interest and engagement to get the prospective customer to actually pick up the phone and call the practice, or even send an email or connect via online chat. The goal is to get the perspective customer on the phone because that is where the practice has the opportunity to convert the prospective customer into a patient or client.

You mentioned you produce videos for clients and that video is important to let potential customers see the actual person they'd be dealing with. Will you please expand on that topic?

Dan Goldstein: Videos are tremendously important right now for a couple of reasons. Number one, videos occupy a huge proportion of the bandwidth and the time that people are spending online. It gives the prospective customer or patient an opportunity to connect with the lawyer or the doctor on a little bit more of a personal level. So, it's not just impersonal text that they read from a page, they actually get a sense whether they can have a rapport with that lawyer or doctor before they contact the practice. Video is hugely important. We have also found it to be extremely important to highlight the phone number and direct the visitors to the website and to make the phone call. We do that graphically by kind of forcing the attention of somebody who is visiting the website to a phone number versus forcing them to a contact form to fill out. We make a big effort at every stage of what we do to really drive the phone calls.

What other things do you put on the website that is going to make people call, that may elicit some kind of trust so that they will make a decision?

Dan Goldstein: The way you design the website and make it user friendly to drive people's attention where you want it to go, is a good starting point. It's also extremely important that you have content that really addresses a prospective customer's interests and needs. Typically, what you want to do is make sure that you are able to answer questions that a prospective customer may have. In doing that, you are demonstrating a level of expertise that builds trust and confidence so that if the customer feels that level of confidence, they are more likely to make the phone call. You can do that with content that is text based, graphical content and with video content and in some cases, a combination. We use infographics, graphic text snippets, that really highlight reasons why somebody on the website would be interested in taking the next step and contact the lawyer or the doctor or the dentist.

Page 1 Solutions, your website, has a pop up after a few seconds. Is that something that you do with your clients' websites?

Dan Goldstein: That part actually refers to a book I wrote a couple of years ago, *Win with Multichannel Digital Marketing,* which is still on point today. Anyone interested in online marketing, it would be worth downloading the free eBook. You can download it directly from my website. I believe that it is valuable content and important for a potential client of mine to understand all the different opportunities they have online and how all those different things work together. It talks about the different channels of online marketing that are out there.

Maybe you did a little search engine optimization and you are done now. You can't stop there because of social media, video paid advertising, display app. There's all kinds of different channels and opportunities for you and so ideally you try to take advantage of the ones that do best that will do best in your particular situation, given your market and your target audience. Now, in terms of do we do that same thing for our clients? In some cases, yes. But to do that, the client really needs to have something meaningful to give away. In this case, what we're talking about is this book that I wrote, when with multichannel digital marketing, I'm not, a lot of our clients have written books like that, so it's a little bit harder to do it. What we do instead though is we've created premium content which is downloadable content that really gets a little bit deeper and further answers questions for that a consumer might have about that doctor or that lawyers practice and the services and procedures that they offer. So what we do there as well, we'll have maybe several white papers or a checklist or some kind of more substantive content that goes beyond what's on the website and in order to get that content the visitor has to provide their email address and that just simply allows for a series of follow up emails by the practice.

Now, as far as getting content on the website, you've mentioned a few times, it's about answering the questions that the clients may be asking themselves. How do you find out what those questions are?

Dan Goldstein: That's actually one of the key pieces there with every single client. We do a tremendous amount of research upfront before we even sign up the client. And then even after we signed them up as we're getting started we're really analyzing data and looking at what queries are being presented by the customers viewing the website. Or even if they're not viewing the website they might be asking questions on Google and the website may be showing up on page two or three for those questions, but not showing up on page one, but we can look through Google search console and get a really good idea of the kinds of questions that Google sees on a regular basis. Then we try to make sure that we have content that answers those questions in a thorough way, preferably content that is more in depth than, and more helpful to a consumer than the client's competitors.

When we do that, we benefit in two ways. First, we provide information that allows Google to see this website has great information. I'm going to display it when somebody puts an inquiry about this topic. The second thing is that when a consumer actually gets to the website, they have an abundance of information that answers the questions that they have. So they're less likely to leave the website and go somewhere else to look for it. It really does come down to researching that information upfront. And then in an ongoing basis. And then the other thing that I would say that comes really a very close second and probably as equally important is making sure that you have content providers who could be done by a written content or it could be done on video or it could be done on social media who really understand the nature of the, have the practice of the, that the website is promoting. In other words, the nature of our clients practice. And so, for that reason, we have a team of writers. We have a team of social media specialists with video. All of these people have specific expertise and knowledge in the very narrow verticals that we target for our clients. And because of that, because we're able to focus on these very specific verticals, our staff becomes pretty expert in what works and what doesn't work in those areas across a number of different cities and markets throughout the country. US and Canada, as I mentioned earlier.

Does Google My Business work well for the doctors, dentists, attorneys for driving phone calls?

Dan Goldstein: The three-pack would be the map listings are what are sometimes referred to as Google places or Google local. The name has changed over time, but yes, that is critical. Basically, the way google organizes its search results as you have the paid AdWords now called Google ads at the very top, usually three, sometimes four listings at the top. Then you have the map with usually three listings on the map. Those are, in my case, lawyer's offices, dental, dental offices, plastic surgery, opposite as ophthalmology offices that are nearby where the where the user is typing in the query and then following that as the organic listings. So, our priority is always to get into that map, into that Google map box and we have a few ways to do it. Obviously, there are organic ways which is traditional search engine optimization. A lot of the things that we do for the organic section, which is immediately below the maps also work to help get our clients higher placement in the maps listing, ideally in the top three. One thing that we do know though is that with maps, location is really key. And if a client is outside of a market, they're less likely to show up in the maps results and they are, if the client is centrally located in the market. So that's a starting point, but it's not the end, it's not the end point. There are some ways to actually get into the maps results through paid listings. We've been able to take advantage of that for some of our clients as well.

How many opportunities are there to get in the organic section, especially with all these directories that seem to be showing up nowadays?

Dan Goldstein: The higher up on the page you are the better. But not everybody clicks on the paid ads, right at the top. In fact, most data shows about 20 percent of viewers actually click on that. The rest, skip over the paid ads go right to the map. And then in some cases they would go right to the organic listings. So, all three are important. It ultimately comes down to a client's budget and how aggressive they want to be to determine where we focus our time and energy. It is all of those are important strategically. Ideally, if you're aggressive, you want to have positions in all three for search phrases that are going to be relevant to your practice,

A lot of times our clients assume that a phrase that they believe is important is something that a lot of consumers type in. The reality is that just because you know a particular practice or a particular type of work really well doesn't mean that you're your target audience, your perspective clients or patients will know that. So, it's important to really get the data upfront as to how people are searching for certain services. It's not always what you assume. In fact, if you look at the high-profile search phrases, in many cases it's, it's phrases that you would never suspect. The other thing that we've found is that targeting a single or even two or three or five specific search phrases only gets you part of the way there to really be effective you need to have content that will show up on a wide range of search phrases related to a particular topic. So, what I like to think about is a word cloud and so where you might have a phrase, I'll use a personal injury lawyer, let's say it's a car wreck attorney. Well, there's are a whole bunch of different phrases that are relevant to that. Car Wreck Attorney may or may not be the one in your market that is searched most frequently, but you want to show up for auto accident where or accident attorney personal injury lawyer or personal injury attorney or accident law firm. I mean there's a whole range of different phrases and some of them might even be things like best accident attorney or something like that. And the only way you really know what is most important is by actually looking at your data. Looking at your Google search console data. Which is really where that is is most relevant and then targeting the targeting the cloud or phrases that are around that specific practice area. That's how you get the most bang for the buck

Does content dictate how you show up in the Map Pack too?

Dan Goldstein: Content is certainly highly important. That's always the starting point, I mean google indexes content and then ranks it based on relevance, but it also ranks it based on how credible it is and one of the ways that it determines credibility is how many other websites actually linked to that specific page or that specific content. So, when you are really, you're really hitting on all cylinders when you have not just great content on your site, but other webmasters, other websites, directories, informational sites, etc. linking back into that page as; here's an authority, here's a resource that you should look at if you're looking for more information. So the starting point is always really deep, rich, meaningful, original content, but that only gets you so far. You still need to have links from other websites pointing to it because that tells Google that your content is actually more valuable than another competitors content.

How much content are you producing for a typical dentist or doctor or lawyer in a month?

Dan Goldstein: That's a great question and it varies so much. We have clients who are in a relatively small market who don't need a lot of content to have a dominant presence in the search results. We have other clients who are in larger markets but already ranking well. They maybe don't need as much on new content, and so what we then do is we really work on improving the quality of the content that is, there adding graphics, adding video and things that are going to improve the conversions from the traffic that they're already getting. But of course, when you have a new practice or a practice that has not done well historically, the starting point, we believe the foundation for all online marketing is really rich deep content that answers those consumers' questions. So, it depends on what stage you are in the practice as to how much you get. We have clients who some months we'll do three, four, five pages for them or blog posts. Some of that content is on their site, some of that content is off their site. In some cases, we'll even do more, some cases we do less and we work on the existing content.

What are some of the myths or misunderstandings about SEO?

Dan Goldstein: Well I kind of alluded to one earlier, which is that a lot of people just assume, hey, there's one big search phrase and if you get that search phrase, you win the battle. Even if you get nothing else. So, you could show up for the phrase personal injury lawyer Denver, for instance. But, a lot of people don't search for personal injury lawyer, Denver, even if you're number one and you may get a fair amount of traffic for being number one in the rankings for personal injury lawyer Denver. But if you also show up for a whole other range of search phrases that relate to the services that you target, other people are searching, in fact, many other people, the vast majority of people are searching for a wider range of search phrase so you end up doing better if you publish a wider net, so to speak, of phrases that are relevant to your practice versus targeting one or two narrow ones.

I think the other thing that I would say most of our clients, particularly new clients, but I think this applies to most businesses. They assume that search engines like a switch, you pay some money, somebody does a few technical mumbo jumbo things on your website and voila, all of a sudden, you've got a top ranked a page on Google and the reality is it's not like that. It is a lot of hard work, research, taking the information you gathered from that research and then applying it and doing that over and over again and working on specific things to improve the rankings, to improve your traffic, to improve your conversions. All those things work together and in some cases, it takes several months, sometimes it takes over a year to really get the full benefit of that. And then you have to keep doing it because your competition is standing still either.

What are some examples of some businesses that you've worked with? What kind of problems that they have when they came to you? What were you able to do for them and ultimately what was the outcome for that business?

Dan Goldstein: We have a number of examples. In fact, we've recently done a study that shows after we've redesigned a client's website, how that's improved traffic and lead generation and those numbers are pretty dramatic. But in terms of a specific story that I can share, several years ago we had a plastic surgery client come to us. That client happened to be in the Denver market and as I mentioned earlier, we cover a lot more than just Denver, but this client happened to be in Denver, which is always nice for us because then we have a lot more face time with the client. But they came to us and asked us to take over their website because it really wasn't performing very well and they weren't happy with their current web marketing provider. What happened was the current web marketing provider at the time got angry and decided to take action in an unethical way and they removed the client's website from the web. This client essentially had initially fairly poor performance overall anyway, but they dropped off the map 100 percent because their website was taken down. We had to recover the website, rebuild it, and then obviously optimize it and get a show up on the search engines. We were able to do that and this particular client, again, it's a plastic surgeon in Denver now dominates, I mean, they are at the top of the search rankings and they do a bunch of other things to generate business from social media to video and all types of marketing. They really took our advice and it's paid off handsomely for them. Now, it's probably been about seven, eight years and they are just continuing to thrive in a very competitive market.

What are some of the questions that a potential doctor, attorney dentists should be asking a digital marketing company to know that they're working with the right ethical company to do the job for them?

Dan Goldstein: That's a good question and I think that a lot of that is just common sense. It's not even about specific questions. You have to be confident that you can trust the people who are going to be working on your website. So, the first thing that I would recommend is that they not just meet with the salesperson, but they actually meet with the rest of the team that'll be working on their So one of the things that we do, and we build it into our contract, is we will give the client an $800 credit to fly out to Colorado and meet with our staff for a day because we believe that if we do that, two things happen. Number one, we get a much better feel for what is important to that client and then we focused all our efforts on trying to achieve those results for that client. Number two. And equally important, the client really gets to understand not just the salesperson or their account manager, but they really get to know the people who are writing content or doing social media or doing the search engine optimization so that they develop a level of trust that is more than just one layer deep. They see that there's a depth of resources to the organization. We have a lot of confidence in our team We have 40 people here and in Colorado and we're really proud of their expertise and I always encourage our clients to come out to learn from them and take advantage of that knowledge. We also have a team in India that does a lot of technical development work for us. And so, we feel really confident in the depth of resources here. And to me that's a crucial piece that any person who is considering hiring a website marketing company, whether it's for SEO or social media or what have you, that they really understand that the people behind the scenes are the ones that do the work and make sure that they have confidence that that team knows what they're doing and is going to be able to get the job done.

What is the best way for people to reach out to you if they need help?

Dan Goldstein: Well, for starters go to our website Page1Solutionscom. You can also email me at DanG@Page1Solutions.com. Or, give us a call at any time. The main number here is **(303) 233-3886**. I'd be happy to answer any questions that you have that would help you in your practice.

About Dan Goldstein

Dan Goldstein is the President and owner of Page 1 Solutions a website marketing firm for attorneys, dentists and doctors.

Dan joined Network Affiliates as General Counsel in 1993 after working as an attorney in Denver and Washington, D.C. In 1994, Dan took over Network Affiliates' Medical Advertising Division. He directed the Medical Advertising Division for approximately 10 years until late 2003. In the mid to late 90s, Dan helped a number of clients develop websites and became interested in website marketing and search engine positioning. Since website marketing began yielding exceptional results for clients, Dan created Page 1 as a joint venture with Network Affiliates. In 2003, he purchased the majority interest in Page 1 from Network Affiliates and turned his full attention to Page 1.

While at Page 1, Dan acquired MegaHunter, LLC as a wholly-owned subsidiary. Dan is also the managing partner of personalinjury.com, which promises to become the leading resource for consumers to find personal injury lawyers and information about personal injury law.

Dan has written numerous articles and given many presentations on Internet marketing at various conferences for attorneys, physicians and dentists. He remains actively involved in the business of Page 1, focusing on research, content development and search engine marketing.

Dan enjoys karate, traveling, hiking, camping and keeping up on current events.

WEBSITE

Page1Solutions.com

PHONE

(303) 233-3886

LINKEDIN

Linkedin.com/company/Page-1-Solutions

EMAIL

DanG@Page1Solutions.com

Empowering Leaders to Release Ineffective Patterns and Habits for Greater Success

Fiona is a Communication Success Strategist and Success Coach; her desire is to guide others and to effectively help communicate their thoughts with clarity and confidence.

In 2014, she went through a major medical crisis and as she laid in the hospital, unable to communicate her needs she was filled with gratitude for those that were there for her in her darkest moments and who could communicate on her behalf. She is forever thankful for her Aunt who was with her that day and was her voice when she could not speak for herself.

Often, we take our lives and our ability to communicate on our own for granted. We think we will always be able to function at the level we are now.

As she looked back on that near-death experience she asked herself these important questions "What if I had never regained my ability to communicate?" "What if I was unable to tell those close to me that I loved them again?" It was a huge wakeup call for her and as she realized how powerful communication is in our lives. When we are unable to or don't have the ability to effectively communicate, it impacts everything we do from our careers to our personal lives. Our ability to communicate could literally be the death of our future career and even our important relationships.

Fiona realized that "If You're Not Effectively Communicating Your Thoughts... It's Literally Costing You Your Future!"

Once she discovered her passion or once her passion found her – she became laser focused on what she knew what it was she was created to do and that is to Motivate and Inspire others to be the best version of themselves. Her company Speak Hope International was born.

"To Know your truth and walk accordingly is being authentic and only then do you really experience what it means to truly live." Fiona Johnson

Conversation with Fiona Johnson

Tell us about your business and the types of clients you're helping

Fiona Johnson: My business, is Speak Hope International, and I am a communication success strategist, and CEO and founder of Speak Hope International and my clients are really people who are at a crossroads that's looking to get to the next stage in their life. They have goals, but they don't know how to get to that next stage. And so, I guide them through that. I also work with companies who are looking to enhance their communication skills within their organization, to see how they can empower their internal and external clients. Those are the people that I work with, people who are up to big things, and just need someone to guide them through the process of it.

Is there a certain age group or demographic that you work with or who exactly is that?

Fiona Johnson: There's not necessarily an age group, but the demographic that I look into are women and men, companies who definitely need to get to that next stage in their success level. When it comes to age I would say starting at 21 because mostly when you're 21 you're, you know what you're about to a certain extent. You've gone through the teenage years and now you're looking to move on to adulthood and generating income and so you want to have the correct tools to get there. So those are the people that I work with.

So how did you get started in this business?

Fiona Johnson: That's a very good question. I've always been passionate about helping people. Having those aha moments or walking into a truth or you know, being authentic to who they are. And there was a situation that happened a few years ago where it was a life changing situation for me personally and I almost missed my opportunity to live out my dream. I went into the hospital for a routine surgery and I ended up in the ICU and when I woke up I realized that my aunt was there. She was the one who was communicating for me and at that moment I recognized how important it is to be able to communicate with people and the importance to articulate where you are in life and what you would like to have happened.

Having gone through that experience I've learned that whatever your dreams are, whatever your goals are, you shouldn't delay those, you should always maximize your opportunities when they come along and do the things that you've set out to do and do the things that you're passionate about, the things that when you go to bed at night, you are always thinking about it and when you wake up in the morning you are thinking about it. That's the passion that you have. And for me, I almost missed that. And so, I'm thankful that I was given a second chance to explore that avenue. And when I started looking into, what is it that I would like to do, knowing that this was my passion, it's just a matter of exploring the opportunity and getting out there, doing the things that I needed to do to get onto the path that I am now. It's been an incredible journey and the clients that I now have, they're on this journey also because they're now wanting to live out their dream and I'm able to help them with that because I've been there, so I can guide them through the process as well.

Was there a book that has influenced you along the way?

Fiona Johnson: *How to Win Friends and Influence People* by Dale Carnegie. When I read it, there was one part, that just resonated with me and one of them was when he always speaks about the importance of how to communicate with people and you never really win an argument and you always want to make it the other person's idea. It's amazing how he was able to capture the essence of good leadership, effective leadership, and communication skills. And when he says no one ever wins an argument, this is true because sometimes we're communicating with our staff or we're communicating with our family and friends and we want to win, but not understanding that there's really no win because if I win the argument, the other person is left feeling bad. How does that make it that we're in a mutual area and you want to always come out where everybody's in a win-win, win situation. So that was one of the books that kind of guided and influenced me through this process here.

A lot of people that I interview, they identify with a person that's inspired them. Do you have someone that's done that?

Fiona Johnson: No one other than the good Lord himself or, you know, the good book, the Bible. But I always listened to Bob Marley from Jamaica and when I listened to him the way how he answers questions, and the fact that he connected with who he is as a person. He's authentically him, he's not trying to be anyone else. And so, for me, looking at how he was able to use that to just be himself and to become the person that he was, even in death. He is more popular probably in death than he was in life. And so, when you think about what legacy you would want to leave, you want to look at people who have left those kinds of legacies and emulate them, and what they have done. And the truth is, if you're being honest with yourself and being real, then people can only accept you for that because they know what they're getting, and they understand the process of where you're coming from. It's easy for them to relate to who you are. So yeah, he was really one of my role models. He is someone that I do look up to and respect.

I've had the pleasure of being around you and I've seen your passion. But what is it that really drives you to help the people that you help?

Fiona Johnson: It's really about the discovery. It's just about people recognizing that they're worthy, and they're valued and that they can be just about anything that they were created to be. Often people are told that they're not going to be successful or they've been beaten down or spoken down to and they feel as though they're worth has been diminished. And for me, it's always wanting people to know their worth and walking them through that process. If you don't know who you are, you'll never know where you're going to go in life, and sometimes because we have never taken the time or no one has ever taken the time to speak with someone or to get to know who they are and to help them get through whatever the obstacles are, or their struggles, they're stuck and for me, if we get them unstuck, for them to get to the place that they need to be, I love to see people achieving and like to see people living out what they were created to be.

What is it that you're finding to be the most common obstacle? Preventing them from being unstuck or not being stuck?

Fiona Johnson: Mostly the obstacles that I run into with my clients is the fear of the unknown. Even though they're not comfortable in that situation, they're just as afraid to take that initial step and open a door because they're fearful of what is behind that door. I always say to them, you know, that's the only way you're going to know. I've come to realize that if you take the initial step, oftentimes there's someone waiting on the other side to help you on your journey. Once people get that concept, I think they're more open to doing what they know they should do and get over that initial hurdle because really, it's the fear.

I was talking to someone yesterday and she said, "I always wanted to be a nurse, but I was afraid of math. I went to my initial class and the professor told me I had the math level of a first grader." Because of that she never went to school. She never became a nurse and she regrets it to this day. And so those are some of the things that when you're talking to people understanding what the biggest obstacle in their life is, it would really be fear.

If they decide that they're going to push through the fear, what would be another pitfall that they might not be aware of?

Fiona Johnson: That's a very good question because when you think about it, if you stay in the situation that you're in, you never know what could have been and because sometimes you're afraid to move out of it because of fear, we get stuck in a situation where they regret, they might not know in the moment you don't see it because you're in it, but years from now you'll look back and you'll have to live with regrets of it. And so that's another pitfall that oftentimes we do not see in the immediate. It will come back to you later in life.

Can you share with us a situation how you've helped someone overcome that?

Fiona Johnson: I have a client and recently she's has been debating, about leaving her current position. She's been in it for a while. Her current position doesn't measure up to where she would like to be and she's not happy. She's looking to work every day and she's just, she's okay, but she's not happy because she knows that's not where she belongs and it was just the fear of getting out there and you know, when we sit there and we go through the process, and you look at the pros and cons because oftentimes you got to way the scale, okay, let's look at this side and the other side. We were able to evaluate the situation and she had decided to step out there and do what she needed to do and be. And now, by the way, she has gotten a job that is now paying her 100 percent more than what she's been paid at her current position. I asked her, what made you do that? Then she said, the one thing you said to me that stood out was, know your worth. And she says, when you said that to me, I had to really think about it. And I knew in my heart the point where I was where I did not belong. And when this opportunity presented itself, she says, I moved, and I unsettled myself. But I went for it. And now I am looking at her and, to be honest, I'm inspired by her. I coached her through it, but I'm inspired by her because I'm having seen where she was coming from and I was witnessing the journey. It's a fantastic story. It's just, for me it just goes to show that the power that we have as human beings to create or own destiny and just go on our path. It's amazing. We just don't know how powerful we are as a people. And so yeah, it's great to see her being successful and doing the things that she knew she was capable of. She's just going to be great.

For people who might be in the same position, what would be your best piece of advice to them?

Fiona Johnson: The first thing I always do with my clients on the discovery process is for them to get clear as to who they are, where they would like to go, what are they looking for? The confusion comes when people do not know who they are. They're not clear what they want, they know they have an idea, but they're not clear. And so for me, it's good for any person to sit down and evaluate where they are in life and to get clear on where they would like to go because once you have an idea as to where you would like to be, me as your coach, all I am there for is to walk you through the process of it and I will guide you through the process of it. But we must have a destination if you don't know where you're going, if it doesn't make sense. So, once you're clear on where you would like to go, and we'll walk you through the process of it.

Some people might say this might not work for me or they're not quite convinced of that. What can you add to help them understand that?

Fiona Johnson: There is a tool that I use that I mentioned from my previous client and I've used it with other clients too. This communication tool that I use measures your communication style, and gives you something tangible to hold in the palm of your hands to look at once you take this assessment where it takes only 15 minutes, to take the assessment and it gives you this report. Once you start looking at the report, it's telling you what your natural styles are, and then we can coach you through that process. But she has used this tool as well. But the client that I mentioned was amazed how accurate this was for her because she was able to look at it and determine how she liked to communicate.

It highlights the areas that they need to work on and then we can go through that process together. But outside of that, for me, it's every individual person that I coach, I do not have the answers for any of them, they have the answers within them. All I'm doing is extracting that and bringing it to the forefront by asking them the powerful question because why are you stuck? it's not the question, but what is causing you to feel like you feel, what's causing you to be in a position that you're in? They have the answers to it and once they're able to get these questions answered, then I'm able to guide them through the process of it. So, for every person I understand that they might be skeptics out there, but I tell you, I can guarantee them that if they do pick up the phone and they call, we can go through that discovery process.

It's free for the discovery process and then we can go through that and they can assess for themselves. It's something that they would like to go on the journey. This is the journey that they would like to go on, but for every person who is looking to be successful in life, they need to understand who they are and how they should be communicating. If you're not effectively communicating your thoughts, it's literally costing you your future, so they need to understand that the moment they're hesitating, it's costing them their future and is costing them their income. It is costing them their family. You know, setting a different foundation for their kids. And the next generation, there's a cost for them. And so, they would want to take up the challenge, you know, what do they have to lose really.

If the readers want to find out more about how you can help them. What would be the best way for them to do that?

Fiona Johnson: They can visit my website, which is www.speakhopeintl.com or they can call me directly at +1-954-991-9155. Or they can email pursuit@speakhopeintl.com and for all the readers if they do call me and reference this book I have a special offer for them as well so they can get a discount towards their communication assessment with a follow-up coaching session.

About Fiona Johnson

Fiona Johnson is CEO and Founder of Speak Hope International, a Best-Selling Author in "Empower Your Life," and has been a featured in the media including interviews and magazines. Fiona is passionate about empowering Leaders, Entrepreneurs and Business Professionals with her step-by-step programs, so they can release ineffective patterns and habits, and quickly and easily achieve greater success in every area of their lives. Fiona holds a Pre-Law Degree; and B.A. in Psychology. She has a life-long commitment to be the Best of the Best, therefore, she also became a Certified Success Coach and DISC Certified Communication Trainer. Fiona ignites the atmosphere with her innovative methods, empowering presence and her commitment to helping others achieve profound results.

WEBSITE
SpeakHopeIntl.com

EMAIL
pursuit@speakhopeintl.com

LOCATION
Tamarac, FL

FACEBOOK
Facebook.com/SpeakHopeIntl

INSTAGRAM
Instagram.com/SpeakHopeIntl

OTHER
LinkedIn.com/in/SpeakHopeIntl

Helping Business Owners Create Financial Freedom Through Marketing

Dr. Paul S. Inselman is a marketing and financial strategist who's considered to be one of the top business lead generators in the country. If you want more leads for your business, then I would highly suggest that you read closely because Paul always has moneymaking nuggets that he shares with many readers. He's the author of *How to Create Financial Freedom Through Marketing Your Business*, which can be found on Amazon. He was also the recipient of the Outstanding Coaches Award in 2014, 2015, 2016 and 2017. He professionally strategizes with and coaches, startup companies, small businesses, and Fortune 500 executives. His specialty, is creating millionaires.

He's been quoted as saying, "If the business owner listens to me, I have never seen a business or a business person that I could not help grow."

Conversation with Dr. Paul S. Inselman

Why do you have such a reputation of being a powerful lead generator?

Dr. Paul S. Inselman: At the end of the day, folks, all you have is your reputation. So, it's vital that you nurture and protect that reputation with everything that you've got because reputation is everything. I think the reason why I have such a positive reputation is because I get asked to talk on great shows like yours and I'm asked to do lectures all over the country. The bottom line as to what has developed that reputation, it's because of the great results that we get for our clients. We help our clients generate more leads than they have ever had in their entire marketing career.

People are sick and tired of spending time and money on AdWords and Facebook and print ads and radio and TV and never getting a return as promised. Understand, I'm not knocking ad words, Facebook, print ads. I use them all. It's just that people are frustrated that they never get a return. And what we do that's different is that we teach our clients how to get leads, but this is the cool thing without spending an additional dime from what they're doing. And I know it sounds crazy and I know it sounds pie in the sky, but when you understand the concepts and the fundamentals of lead generation and marketing, seriously, it becomes like child's play.

Your title of Marketing and Financial Strategists is an interesting title. Can you describe what you do and how you do it?

Dr. Paul S. Inselman: We analyze local and global markets and we notice trends. We then teach our clients how to create a market dominating position. And we couple that with the use of the conversion equation, which is to interrupt, engage, educate, and offer. And then what we do with our clients is we create custom created goals and custom created plans that are going to get them from point a to point z. We get on the phone each week or a couple of times a week with our clients, whatever's needed. And we basically help them to deploy their plan. We hold them accountable to doing the things that they say they're going to do. And like you said mentioned earlier, we helped to create millionaires this year alone, this quarter alone, we have three or four that have converted to millionaire status. And it's something that's exciting because when you give somebody financial freedom and you couple that with freedom of time, in other words, time to enjoy their money, time to enjoy their family. I'll tell you, man is no greater feeling on the planet for me.

Can you share how the readers can improve their present marketing efforts to get more leads?

Dr. Paul S. Inselman: Every business owner out there right now asks this, why should somebody give you their hard-earned money? What makes you so special that somebody would want to go to you instead of to your competitor? If you're a dentist and Mr. and Mrs. Potential patient is driving down main street and they see a dentist, and dentist B and dentist C, why should they go to your office? If you're a lawyer or a chiropractor or an accountant, the same thing if you're a plumber and electrician or any other tradesmen. The same question why somebody should go to you if you're stumped and you can't answer that question, that's a problem, and it must be corrected. The way we correct it is we help our clients to determine what their market dominating position is. And if you have a market dominating position, you never ever have to compete on price again.

Let me give you an example. I'm an apple vendor and I have apples for sale and I have red delicious apples for sale. You touch them, and you feel them, and they feel identical. You smell them, they smell identical and they have a deep red color. The apple on the left is fifty cents and the apple on the right is $1. Based on the information that I just gave, you know, if I asked somebody which one they would buy, the answer logically is the fifty-cent one. It's not a trick question and the reason why are because we would be insane to spend more money based on the information I just gave and myself included. I would buy that fifty-cent one also, but now I'm going to give you more information. The apple on the right, that's an organically grown apple and not only is it organically grown, but we grow it in super soil which boosts the vitamin A and the vitamin C content a thousand times.

In addition to that, we triple wash them in an organic solvent to take off all the residue. So, when I ask people, you know, which would you buy? Now obviously, the dollar one. Now understand not everybody wants an organic apple and that's okay. It's not for everybody, but most people will want the organic apple because quite frankly it's better. It's healthier and it's safer for you and they're more than willing to pay a dollar two times as much as the standard apple. That is an example of market dominating position that organic apple will fetch more money. It never has to compete on price, and more people will want it than not, and you've now increased your profits and you've increased your position in the community. Let's translate that to the dentist, to the Chiropractor, to the plumber, to the lawyer, the accountant. When somebody's going down main street, what's going to make them say, ah, that's an organic apple instead of a regular apple.

What makes that chiropractic practice stand out? What makes that dentist stand out? That's how we help our businesses get more leads by first creating that market dominating position. The next thing that we do is we use that conversion equation, which is interrupt, interrupt as your headline. Then engage, engage the sub headline. Then we educate people. We educate them on why your market dominating position is better than everybody else. It positions you to be the best and then a compelling offer. let me give you an example. Why would somebody want to use me for my services? And the answer is simple. I'm not going to give you platitudes of telling you how great I am. I'm going to prove to you why we are different and, in my opinion, better than our competitors and the reason is because we have a full line academy that teaches all these things that we're talking about in a video format.

Number two, I have 32 years of business experience and I'm still in business and I know how to grow businesses because this is what we do. The next thing that makes us different is that we are accessible virtually 24/7 and you can compare this with anybody else out there that does, you know, lead generation and business coaching and you will find that our resume and our skills and our ability to be contacted it far exceeds others. Now you can, believe it or not, it doesn't matter. You know, you're not in our world and you haven't experienced it yet, but the fact that we have these programs that separates us and that's what creates our market dominating position.

Business owners get bombarded daily with, you got to do Facebook ads, you got to do Instagram, you got to do YouTube. What do you think is the best marketing medium to use for a small business owner?

Dr. Paul S. Inselman: I am asked that question almost every single day. You know, Hey Paul, what's the best thing to do? And my answer is thinking of marketing like dating. You want to go on a date? What's the best way to go on a date? Do you go out to dinner? Do you go to the movies? Do you go for a quiet walk on the beach? What do you do? They all work every single one because certain people may want to walk on the beach instead of going to the movies, other people may want to find meal instead of eating at home. My point is Facebook. It's awesome ad words. It's awesome. Print ads. They're awesome. Radio TV check. Awesome. Awesome. Postcards. Check. Awesome. Valpak check. Awesome. They're all awesome. My point is it's not the medium. It is two things, number one, the market dominating position and then the message that you're going to deploy, and the other thing that separates us is that we use strategic based marketing, and this is not just a buzzword.

This is a reality. You see, most people use what are called tactical based marketing methods or single step marketing. What that does is it tries to jump a person from point a to point z. let me give you an example. Somebody wakes up today and they've had back pain for 20 years and uh, they just don't want to deal with it anymore. They didn't wake up today saying, Oh, I'm going to get rid of my back pain. I'm going to call Dr. Joe Smith, chiropractor, or Dr. Tim, a physical therapist, or go to an orthopedist. They didn't say that. What they said is, I'm getting rid of my back pain today. They're not ready to call that specific doctor. So that specific doctors advertising a free exam or free consultation, they don't want to talk to that person at that point in time when they woke up, really saying is that they want to research it.

They don't know who they want to go to. You see everybody has a conversation. Every prospect has a conversation's going on in their head and it can be distilled into two things. One, they have something they don't want and two they want something they don't have. So, in this example, the person that's waking up with back pain, they have back pain, they don't want that, and they want something they don't have. They want to be able to play golf. But at this juncture, at this very morning when they woke up, they don't know if they want a chiropractor and orthopedist and massage therapists and acupuncturists or any other discipline. So now they're going to scour the internet or they're going to scour Facebook or they're going to scour ad words hitting google or they're going to look in there Valpak and they're going to look for different disciplines.

And what they are looking for that point in time is information. The reason why I say that all of the mediums are fantastic is because they all work the whole idea is you have to craft the message based on that market dominating position and you have to create strategy. Now, the difference between strategy and tactical based marketing and strategy will shepherd or walk a person from point A to point B to point Z when they're ready to buy. What it takes into account is that people buy at different times. In other words, most people are future buyers. Then they become soon to be buyers and then fewer than one percent of the population are now buyers. A now buyer is somebody who's hungry, wants pizza, they go onto the internet, they find a coupon, boom, I buy pizza a now buyer is somebody who broke down at 11:00 PM on the side of the road they're not looking for a coupon for $10 off their next towing service. They're looking for who gives 24/7 service. This is an emergency. So, my point is, is that you have to understand that people in different parts of the buying cycle, they may be a future buyer as soon to be or a now buyer, strategy allows you to shepherd that person wherever they are, step by step until they're ready to buy from you.

So, to recap, in my opinion, all the mediums are phenomenal. You must use them in the right time, but more importantly is you must craft the right message. And this is why I made that big bold statement earlier, that we are able to help our clients achieve more leads than they ever dreamed possible without spending an additional dime. It's because 99 percent of people out there have learned about marketing, but everything they learned is wrong. What we do is we simply teach them the right way of doing it, and then we go in and we correct their website, we go in and we correct their ad words. We go in and we correct their Facebook so they're not spending an additional dime. They're just creating that market dominating position, using the conversion equation and changing the verbiage properly and then suddenly like magic, they start to get a huge return and that's what's exciting to me.

I'm sure the listeners on the edge of their seats right now, what would be the best way for them to contact you and how can I do that?

Dr. Paul S. Inselman: There are a couple of websites that they can go to. The first is academyofcreativemarketing.com They can also go to www.creativecoachingllc.net or if they want to call us, we work internationally. We just got our first client from Dubai, which is cool. They can reach us at one 888-201-0567.

And I learned something interesting. If somebody is listening in Dubai and wants to reach me, you can't call me through the phones and they can't use skype. You have to use an app called bottom. And that's how we converse with people from Dubai, they've outlawed skype there and all that neat stuff. We also offer some free webinars on how you can get more leads than you can humanly handle. And, if you email me, I can give you that schedule. And these webinars are really, really, in my opinion, powerful, very educational. And my email address is drinselman@creativecoaching.net

About Dr. Paul S. Inselman

Dr. Paul S. Inselman is a sales and marketing strategist, Paul understands how to help clients increase their revenues and dominate their market.

With over 32 plus years of business experience, Paul has helped hundreds of healthcare professionals and small business owners just like you, understand how to capture market share, expand sales, train staff, and become organized.

As a certified behaviors analyst, he has trained hundreds of people on the use and monetization of the language of Disc.

From 2008-2017 Paul's clients saw their income grow on average 165%, with some businesses seeing a double and triple in sales; while according to CNN health care practitioners were down on average 15% and small business grew 4.9%. You will learn how to dominate your market based on sound business principles that work in any economy.

WEBSITE

AcademyOfCreativeMarketing.com

EMAIL

drinselman@creativecoachingllc.net

LOCATION

Coral Springs, FL.

FACEBOOK

Facebook.com/DrInselman

TWITTER

Twitter.com/EnzymeDocPaul

OTHER

LinkedIn.com/in/Paul-S-Inselman-dc-market-and-financial-strategist-65116012/

Entrepreneur | Visionary | Philanthropist

Currency from Heaven - In Partnership with a King

"Seek first the kingdom of God and His righteousness, and all these things shall be added to you." Matthew 6:33

Shawna Ranae is the CEO of a credited and fully licensed Insurance Company, IMO, and Brokerage Firm specializing in Life, Health and Medicare Products.

Shawna is a Strategic Strategist, Visionary, Philanthropist, President for Non-Profit, Chamber of Commerce Member, Business of Zion Partner, Business Developer, writer, philosopher, evangelist, mentor, motivational speaker, Inventor for a Copyright Patent, Investor, Volunteer, Trainer, Event Specialist, Marketing Specialist, Financial Planner, Bible enthusiast, Mother and Entrepreneur.

Shawna has a bachelor's degree in Finance from Southern Illinois University.

Conversation with Shawna Ranae

Please introduce yourself.

Shawna Ranae: My name is Shawna Ranae, I am 32 years old, and I live in Dallas Texas. I was born and raised in a small town right outside of Carbondale, Illinois in where I lived most of my life growing up. My mother, Angela, still resides in Illinois with the rest of my family. My Father, Albert was born in Cabo Rojo, Puerto Rico and raised in Manhattan New York. I also have three siblings to account for: Cody, Ruben, and Lisa. I am a very blessed mother of two beautiful children. A daughter, Madilyn Juliet, in whom has grown into a beautiful young lady with power and strength, she is also a wonderful Violist. Following 11 years later, my son, Nicolas Preston who is the most talented baseball player and follower of Christ. They are my greatest delight and the apple of my eye. I want to thank you Madi & Nico, for always supporting me as your Mother and trusting I will lead us into the way of Everlasting.

We have grown not only as a family but a solid team, and by doing this, we have now declared victory over our generation that will last into Eternity. As we journeyed into our lives together, it wasn't always easy, but you have both grew carefully positioning your wingtips through our trials and synced your wings without regard, flapping, even when I wasn't sure what lied ahead, presumably catching my draft as your mother by simply following me to our inheritance.

May you both always continue to lead by faith, never ceasing and watching as your own destiny unfolds for his glory, always looking onward and upward into the challenges that lies ahead. *Isaiah 11:1-3*

Tell us your thoughts on Leadership

Shawna Ranae: "The Spirit of the Lord will rest on him, the Spirit of Wisdom, Understanding, the Spirit of Counsel and Might, the Spirit of Knowledge and Fear of the Lord" Team work makes the Dream work! Partnership!!

By mediating on God's word, I have learned several ways to implement a strategic strategy for a long-term result. Looking back my "first" true role and test in Leadership came when I became a mother and head of my household. Leadership is defined as being in the state or position of being a leader then in Hebrew "Listen & Repeat." In the earliest days of the Old Testament, the leadership of the people of God was by the family head or patriarch, to whom God spoke his messages. Jesus establishes a connection with us to Himself through the Holy Spirit to help us through our lack of experience. As we watch and listen for His guidance, we grow closer to him through his living word, we start to materialize through scripture our purpose and can even begin to create, align, sow and manifest it on earth.

As I saw this process, I started losing the law of parenting tradition and rules, and everything I knew must be put aside, no longer living under the law of the world, but under his gift of Grace. This became a breeding ground for our success! I learned to allow my children to help me speak into our path and have expressed input for everyone's good. This method became very beneficial to me and made our home empowered and our fueled kingdom confidence by helping us rely on the truth. All though all things must be tested we know what we know and in living by Grace. Grace removes the borders of resistance and allows us to push through the walls that block our path. See our children were keys and little helpers administrated under the holy spirit to also have a set of eyes to see and ears to hear. I stopped silencing them and putting them under the law of age but instead allowed them elbow room to grow into this change with me, on their terms, then we measured it out together to see what was to come. Success is never just about us but more about our presence and what we have to give to help bear more fruit in the situation. Making everyone a part of the process embraces the next step for the reward. Leaders evaluate decisions generationally, now and later. The first step into changing the world is to start at home. Making sure we all reach our pinnacle of success by engaging ourselves completely changes Nations.

When Madilyn was growing up, she brought this certain kind of standard into our home. She forced me to realize in my failure to fulfill her needs as a child with a voice; I learned to stop living through her to make myself feel better and grew to learn we were separate people and she had her own destiny that should be evaluated through our decisions. Yes, I was her mother, and yes, I was in charge, but I had to realize Madilyn (children) are born as Nation, and I was just the administer of her seed who would be forever connected. When we embrace our position, we can help those we love the most and spending our time with aligning with their own destiny, are a role in incubating is only to love and to nourish so the pattern can repeat itself successfully. When we let people rise knowing it can fell takes COURAGE & great inner STRENGTH to come into fulfillment with our support as parents.

Leadership is about knowing your worth and speaking it out. This all becomes very rewarding when we allow room for more choices, then communicating through the mistakes or watching people succeed and believe in themselves. The rule in our home is, we are allowed to make them, but with that choice, we also have to be responsible for dealing with the outcome. No of us are perfect, and we must be allowed to fail so we can grow naturally into the next level. My son Nicolas adapted very quickly on this strategy, even as a toddler, he was taught to continue through the process and make the right choices for the right reason.

Leaders are born through opposition and secure themselves by learning from their failure, treating it as a gift which allows them to build a foundation on a rock, this is my definition of freedom. We effectively choose the right decisions, for the right reasons for living by faith and trusting our way through the unknown. Wisdom; the gift that silences the ignorance of foolish men, the one that surfaces as supreme. The results of this effective leadership in our home have been astonishing. I will share a special story with you later in this chapter that will prove this blessing to you... My thoughts on leadership is about fruit and living your whole life more abundantly. My greatest inspiration has come from my children and watching them create and innovate their own ways through life independently with me right by their side helping them secure a legacy.

Tell me about your early career

Shawna Ranae: In my early career, I sold life and health insurance only. Entrepreneurs are drawn to the hustle and making money by their results. Even as a child, I was very independent, resourceful, driven and my desire for problem-solving always allowed me to reach my peak. I grew up very poor, so naturally, I was hungry for success, and completely sold out for the Industry. I've watched and learned from several great leaders like Zig Ziglar, Dale Carnegie & Napoleon Hill how to feed my vision and I ran with it in excitement. Thankfully, I've been mentored by some of the best, some in which were multi-million-dollar a year salary earners who see the best in me, even before I couldn't see it, they could coach me though. You will eventually become the company you keep – The sign to watch for is their Fruit, Matthew 7:15 says you will know them by their fruit. Not money, evaluate the areas in where you are prospering. Being equally yoked will make you, or break you, but your Passion will Lead you. The day I decided to get my Insurance License, I knew I was on a date with destiny, and my life would never be the same, my passion drives me here, and it always inspires me home from my failure. I'm a people person, and I enjoy seeing our sales results and watching the numbers grow while clients are being protected.

Most importantly, I believe in what I do, and this allows me to minimize the competition by knowing we offer only the best the market has to offer. Passion pulls you to the top, and it helps me lead instinctively every day on purpose. The words "Act" and "Instinctively" have brought me some of the best months in business. As I ushered myself into this lifestyle of a non-routine schedule, spirit lead, self-discipline and obedience by habit, it created an automatic alignment in everything I am today. It wasn't until I learned my gift of faith to understand how to unlock my destiny by knowing the right keys to use, mechanical obedience isn't sufficient, we must do and live on divine purpose. I love the story about Jacob in his early year of Success found in Genesis 28: 11-16 We see; Jacob created a ladder to the heavens through his vision, and later this was a key that opened the door into his inheritance by God meeting him in a certain place. Jacob took one of the stones from that place and put it at his head, and he lay down in that place to sleep. Then he dreamed, and behold, a ladder was set up on the earth, and its top reached to heaven, and there the angels of God were ascending and descending on it. And behold, the LORD stood above it and said: "I am the LORD God of Abraham your father and the God of Isaac; the land on which you lie I will give to you and your descendants. Also, your descendants shall be as the dust of the earth; you shall spread abroad to the west and the east, to the north and the south; and in you and in your seed all the families of the earth shall be blessed. Behold, I am with you and will keep you wherever you go and will bring you back to this land; for I will not leave you until I have done what I have spoken to you." Then Jacob awoke from his sleep and said, "Surely the LORD is in this place, and I did not know it." I want you to pray you don't miss these invitations of Revelation along your path to destiny, it's important we lead with a pure heart, so we can see the invisible into our future, times in your early career will give you clues on how it will all end.

What has been a key to your success?

Shawna Ranae: The key was to *Believe, by faith* in his promises and hold God accountable to his word! I knew that whatever career I choose if I met the conditions I would make it, it was written. I told myself there was no plan B, and I would have to burn the boat when I got to dry land and continue into what I believed for. The key is to Never Give Up. If your passionate about what you do, carry integrity and speak in truth, it is a promise you will succeed, and money will start to work for you. God's word was the key to all my success, the truth aligned and gifted me all that I needed. It created in me an eternal banking account from Heaven with our names on it. The keys were Knowledge, Wisdom, Understanding and a double Portion of the Fear of the Lord. Then It was credited to me. Think of all the angels on Jacobs ladder in his dream, could you imagine an organization which is Administrated through perfect Justice, Peace and Truth working for your good by succession just because you believed! The Key is Faith and Righteousness is our reward, it is a gift from God, just like Grace is a Gift, it's our Redemptive Right to be Successful, and we must learn to tap into. I was raised that money was the only key but keys don't have a voice and money has a voice, and goes where you tell it to go, therefore making it a defense and not a key. Establishing and Keeping a Covenant with God is the keeper of my master key.

Tell us about who inspired and influenced your style of leadership?

Shawna Ranae: My mother was a factory worker almost all my life, she flourished in her profession despite her wage. This trait of discipline was remarkable and very important for me to see growing up. Regardless of how she accepted the position, I could have never imagined her working in a commission-only job, going into to homes she didn't know and calling leads for the hustle of a dollar. I guarantee that would have been entirely out of the question.

Naturally, I wasn't a born leader and growing up I repelled discipline so, at some point, I had to be humbled. I was never taught how to run a race in business, let alone how to be an entrepreneur, so all my success seemed to have come with the price of my pride. In a certain place of my life, I had to make a choice to show up, connect, then build the relationships for a stake in the equity. Entrepreneurs work for freedom, and I heard the only color they have seen was green. However, that way is not the only way, and for the everyday blue-collar commonality type was working a 9-5 is just as great if you are aligned with your calling. Entrepreneurs may seem to build the cities, but you maintain it; therefore, we are all in partnership.

When we read in the Bible, God always blessed generational. He never seemed to have a favorite, and just when you think he does, he ends the blessing with all and passes it around the table. Praise God for that! How exciting, if we met the conditions, we get to partake in the everlasting covenant. Unfortunately for some, we may have been taught, Christians aren't wealthy, and that is precisely what I thought until I met my new partner. The truth is, we all desire greatness and everyone wants to be a leader, and quite frankly, the dream is free, so we all have the same chance in being one. Therefore, we can all lead, but if no one is following you, then we're not leaders anymore, we're followers. Leading at an incredible rate that grows us continually into character, by culture through volume, in peace is nothing less than a great reward. Our job as leaders is maintaining a good attitude which is nourishment, followed by persistence which is accountability and type of discipline.

We must find the importance in knowing how to keep and maintain our lot, and to know our field by studying truth, then implementing it into your daily physical life like a farmer, sowing seeds. Studying my bible teaches me how to watch and hear the unseen through parables. Jesus emphasizes and confirmed several times these great principals in the Bible for us today, through our accounts from Heaven and personal example from his statement in Matthew; The law won't get you into heaven, as nor will product or money make you rich in business. However, the exception and order through this exchange who was speaking about to give you a key to a special type of currency. In the Beatitudes, Jesus spoke in parables through the sower in which I now base a personal business principle on every day, Matthew: 13: 18-22

"Then He spoke many things to them in parables, saying: "Behold, a sower went out to sow." and as he sowed, some seed fell by the wayside; and the birds came and devoured them. Some fell on stony places, where they did not have much earth; and they immediately sprang up because they had no depth of earth. But when the sun was up they were scorched, and because they had no root they withered away. And some fell among thorns, and the thorns sprang up and choked them. But others fell on good ground and yielded a crop: some a hundredfold, some sixty, some thirty."

Tell us more about the dream you had and how it impacted your life?

Shawna Ranae: When God showed me these words in a dream (The Beatitudes) which was a year before I moved to Texas, I had no idea what he was talking about nor did I implement them. It wasn't until my move; another year later was I able to see and hear what he was saying for me in business. This parable is about sowing a seed which grows from the relationship for our everyday lives through him, in business.

For those of you who deal with people every day, think about your clients. As you visualize, interact and listen, you will understand this seeding process, which must take root for a harvest. Use these parables, through the situations, with your clients; then you will see it activate. Leadership is about sowing a seed with emotion in complete obedience to profit. Teaching, then doing! Wow! That's powerful, right! Let me show you more. Some of the most influential leaders in my life have always put their need for superiority aside and proved their success to me by leading from the front or showing me through his word how to plant.

I walk behind great leaders, who are very influential, like Doris Wagner who was the wife of Peter Wagner, Barbara Wenthroble, who wrote a book about "Accessing the Power of God" then Linda Heidler, who wrote the book "The Apostolic Woman" and lastly, Chuck Pierce who is now my amazing pastor and wrote several fantastic books, My personal favorite is called: "A Time to Advance."

Successful influencers will equip you along the way. These tremendous leaders in front of me feed me the word and later I will introduce you personally to a legacy. Leaders don't just lead the pack; they join them. If you think about it, compassion won't ever allow you to sit on the bench, so why wait for tomorrow? I've watched as some of the most successful people despite their titles will always take time out to develop you or take time out for themselves by consistently pouring into areas that were lacking for improvement by staying coachable and self-disciplined to master their craft. Impactful people are givers and never look for a return.

When we discipline ourselves to act in obedience by recognizing our problems only to rise above them, we instinctively start to improve our standards without realizing it. We start emotionally paying our dues in time, commitment and discipline for the result by faith redeeming our award. Anytime this happens: you know your seed will eventually breakthrough, you will start looking for the voice of God in everything you do because you will feel him near.

Abraham and Jacob were greatly blessed in the Bible, but if you notice, right before the blessing came, they heard Gods' voice then they both did two things. Number 1: they acknowledged their resource, and Number 2. They committed in a vowed to pay their tithes. Whether you are a Christian or not, we all walk by this principle, but only a few embrace it. Yes, you must pay your tithes, but God doesn't want your money, he wants you! Committed adhesion to him for the result of your good is the catalyst for succession and will complete you by the process. Let God work you from the inside out...

Tell us about how important mentors have been to you on this journey?

Shawna Ranae: God's word is my Portion and my Cup.
Without my mentors, it would have taken me longer to discipline myself in knowing how to capitalize my resources in this way, before my success I kept myself very busy marinating most of the time in what I already knew thinking I was making a difference and that was a big mistake. To learn this mixture in the aroma, I had to bring the knowledge I was

given from above, on the road with me and dig! Train yourself to get to the source and where there is no way, create one.

To be an Entrepreneur it takes a different kind of boldness to succeed, and often I will investigate the person to know the root of their understanding or where their heart is, for everything must matter, even a person's name has great significance. "If all of it doesn't matter, none of it does." I think it's very important to know who is leading you, no matter what kind of job you have so you know it's true. This way of seeing plows yourself into the better ground and gives you the reasons as to why you are to challenge yourself. If you are planting a garden, don't you want to know what your planting!

"Don't ever take advice from someone you are not willing to trade places with." A good farmer knows what lies beneath. I want to encourage anyone who is taking the time out to read my story to be strong in your morals and values really, you are the most important person in the world, and sometimes where you may be challenged by a manager or mentor, you lack the confidence you need to stand up for yourself, and that's okay, always do the right thing for the right reasons, and chose peace.

Many times in my career I had incompetent bosses, or greedy leaders and lacked the resources I needed to carry myself without credibility, but my obedience in doing a job well done wasn't about them, it's about you. You owe it to yourself to be thorough at all times never wavering in faith. Create this level of respect for your peers and raise your standard. By drawing this measuring line, you will envelop your authority by your presence alone. Peace is supernaturally supercharged in the outlet of respect. Even those people over you who seem non-in-void can become our biggest blessing, or more importantly, you being their's. "He changes the times and the seasons, he removes kings and raises up kings. He gives Wisdom to the wise and Knowledge to those who have understanding." Daniel 2:21

Mark Cuban is a registered billionaire and has created massive success in business but is always talking about timing. When and how it affects his season for success. Without knowing the importance of this, you may miss your breakthrough. Times and season are the most vital for any farmer, and the Bible was founded on time. Ecclesiastes 3:1 "To everything there is a season, A time for every purpose under heaven. If you read further in Ecclesiastes, you will see what I mean."

When I originally started in business I didn't lead this way, and I never put God first in my life, and I failed greatly because of it. In his unfailing love, I now see he was always putting the right people at the right time into my path to fulfill his purpose in me. Praise God for his will and not our own, give him Authority over your life and hold him accountable by his word. The greatest thing about his word is it never changes, and it never fails. Years can go by, and we change continuously, but when God speaks, when he gifts us, it's irrevocable. When I was a little girl, I couldn't wait to grow up and get a job and now watching my children grow, I feel the need to gently put my children to weed their garden, slowly implementing their seed for instinctive action when they grow up, because I had no idea how much work it was going to take. God said he spoke nations into our seed so why wait 16-18 years for a settlement. Our father has great confidence in us, even as a seed to grow into fulfillment.

As we continue to grow through this chapter together through faith, I pray you will see the final picture for your own special gift from God himself and may he clothed you with Rich Robes. Use my words to leverage yourself during this time and rise above the distraction. As the angel of the Lord removes our filthy garments, we must prepare for a feast.

Tell us about some of your greatest struggles you have faced?

Shawna Ranae: In 2014, I was faced with some of the greatest struggles in my life, in business and my marriage. Growing through these things really challenged me to be who I am today. Naturally, when we are in pain, we reflect or look back for comfort to where we came from, in hope by Wisdom we will know the answer to escape it. As a baby, I started going to church with my grandma, who gave me my name and just turned 70 years old this year. In our journey together, one year I even received the Holy Ghost at just age 10.

But growing up, I started resenting religion, his word, and religious people. They all seemed so out of order to me, and by seeing this, instead of finding God myself, I lost my way. I assumed those people knew the truth and never even challenged the fruit. Even as an adult, Yes, I continued to attend church regularly in routine, but my life didn't carry much substance. I was young, beautiful and ambitious, but I was broke! To fix myself, I grew self-seeking and dependent on myself for an award through my achievements. Testimonies at church and prayers were far from my concern at this point and to hear Gods voice didn't relate to me at all, the same way I came in, the same way I went out.

My greatest success in business didn't come until things fell completely apart. All my life I thought I knew Jesus because I associated with the things that involved Religion and I even had proof, I had been going to church since I was a little girl. I knew his name, his stories and that wrong way of thinking seemed to have awarded me into a place of lies and deception. The truth was, I never read my Bible, I only went by what I was told. Therefore, I could never challenge what I heard and greatly deceived, the exception was that I prayed when there was an issue but that's it. My title as a "Christian" was strong, but the true test was about to come. Praise God for the Spirit of Revelation! This time in my life was one of the worst, and it stormed and rained, and stormed and rained, but God had a plan for me.

Later that year, I was introduced to one of the greatest mentors of all time in my life, his name was Robert Hagan, who now resides in New Haven, CT. Robert wasn't just a businessman; he was a prophet. When I was introduced to him, I was a little intimidated by his title, but I was desperate for a word from God. In return, he ended up being the greatest mentor anyone could ask for, but most importantly I never heard him say he was a prophet. I remember when I first initiated the thought of Texas, he and his wife Katey, bought me a round-trip plane ticket to Texas from Illinois so that I could put myself to rest about it and marinate in my vision to be sure this was what I wanted to do. Robert was the kind of Mentor that brought Life to Gods word and taught truth in how to read the scriptures that sowed into my heart; it pushed me willingly and eagerly straight to Jesus. This created glory over my life, it gave myself authority, and I have seen results. I spent a whole year, personally humbling myself and praying, fasting and growing in the seed of God's word until I knew which path to take. Then one day, it all passed, the truth had set me free. This type of mentorship was very key to my success, it rebuilt my foundation and taught me how to fight for it. Good success is earned by being a farmer, a warrior and an Obedient Student If Life. When a champion runs a race, he never looks over to see who's beating him. Your biggest competitor is yourself.

What makes a great leader in business?

Shawna Ranae: When I reevaluated all the great leaders in business, I noticed theater all pointed us back to our creator. This is Leadership! His word guarantees us eternal success. If we vision the Word Eternal, what happens? You breakthrough, and Go Beyond!

Kingdom leaders get their instructions from a King. It, not a profession, it's a lifestyle. This should be our stand and our rock! Always looking onward and upward, Looking to God for everything has given me access, and keys to our inheritance. Furthermore, as a leader it's important to know the other opponent's standard as well, when measured for a race, or eleven a weight in for a boxing match, you must meet the conditions. We all have different levels of success and what it takes to get there. By his blood, Execution wins them all. Whether you want to make 100k, 200k, a million or even a billion, you must get real with yourself and take action; you can't hit a target you don't see.

So many times, we see new people in business wanting to make the dream a reality, but the seed isn't processed. Example; If you have only made 100k in your life and say you want to make a million, how do you get there? Process! This is why we fail. We skip the process to claim the award. You must walk in stages to know how to maintain it, no matter how far you go. Appreciate your process, it's sowing your seed.

Then when this is complete, raise your standard for the next level, this envelops us the credibility to achieve the goal.

What is the secret to success in business?

Shawna Ranae: The greatest secret in business isn't the pulling from the universe and "imagining" your way to the top, by pretending to make it happen, but it's the connection and the relationship it takes to get there. Personally, I've never been one to want a lot of money or materialistic things, but I work for my freedom and all these things have helped me obtain my goal. I excelled because Confident Leaders introduced me to other Leaders and taught me how to use my resources.

These acts of commitment, equip us for a lifetime. Could you imagine owning a house, without the deed? Can you discern the lie in that sentence? It's impossible to "own" a house without the correct filing. The ability to exercise your resources by Wisdom, Knowledge & Understanding it will change you. The next level of my life is what I like to call "Heavens Currency" the account or price it cost for sacrifice. I will be talking more in detail about this when my book is released in 2019.

"To know Wisdom and Instruction to perceive the words of understanding, to receive the instruction of Wisdom, Justice Judgement and Equity." - Proverbs 1:2

What do you admire in Leadership?

Shawna Ranae: I admire the sacrifice it took a great leader in business to succeed, perseverance is magnetizing. Looking at some of our greatest leaders sacrifice for the sake of our rights, the people and what they believed was awakening. Martin Luther King and John Kennedy were even assassinated, but they died for what they believed in. Watching another sermon or motivational video would never be enough, when you become equipped, you have to use your tools. After losing almost everything, I made a decision to move to Texas and restart my life from the bottom up.

In 2016, my mom successfully recovered from cancer; I got my divorce, then God showed me a vision of what I believed was to come. After God spoke, it was confirmed in my heart, and I knew if I could overcome the obstacle of leaving everything I knew behind and get back to what I loved doing if I only believed! My children and I would have the ability to restore everything that was taken from us and leave a legacy. By moving, I could create more wealth, and we could build more opportunity than where we were currently. The value started measuring up.

That week the door of opportunity presented its self for action, but if I went, I would have to decide quickly. The day it came for us to go I had spent all my money on a U-Haul which only left us with a full tank of gas and $65 to my name to continue. In the natural I was taken the greatest risk by doing this and personally terrified, but I wasn't looking at the risk, but my eyes were fixed on the promise. By going beyond, generationally, I was willing to sacrifice myself to everything I knew by FAITH of making it happen. At this point, the odds were 50/50. I prayed, continuously and Even asked God to personally give me checkpoints in our journey after we leave so I would not be engulfed by the snares and fail. I knew my support would be very little, but My faith in God was bigger. Every time I heard the songs Oceans by Hillsong, I told God if he would play it, I would know it was for me, and no matter what was going on or where I was, I would give him thanks and appreciate where I was, the process and continue to the finish. Long story short his word was alive and true, and the end result to this story is my testimony.

What happened next?

Shawna Ranae: By Covent Faith, Love & War. After only one year of our move, we closed the year out with over $162k in sales, gave several people new jobs and even won an award. My son Nicolas the "decision maker" even landed a partnership with a local company in the Dallas area which later enabled us to open our second business which has become my favorite of the two, a nonprofit advancing our community in youth leadership and restoration. Being a leader hasn't always been great, it's hard work, but surrounding yourself with the right people make it rewarding, along with Truth, Love, Peace & Wisdom, you will see your cup running over. To me, Service is Leadership. Laying yourself down so another may have a chance and sharing your success with those you love the most. My children and I are now slaves to his righteousness, and we will forever know our portion and our cup.

What projects are you working on?

Shawna Ranae: My entire story will be published in 2019, titled "Heavens Currency"

My books go more in detail about these Covenant Promises and How to "unlock" this Free account in heaven which we can pull down, then activate it on Earth for Eternal Reward. Until, we meet again remember your source by breaking bread, in Partnership with the King! Courage and Strength belong to God. Wealth and Riches belong to God. Life & Death Belong to God. So, when you choose to fight the good fight of faith for your inheritance, may you always remember the promise and live completely on your Faith.

Any closing thoughts?

Shawna Ranae: Now as we close, let me introduce you to Joshua; so, you may meet the conditions to have the Strength & Courage for days ahead to Go beyond your borders for Empowerment!

"Now, therefore, arise, go over this Jordan, you and all this people, to the land which I am giving to them—the children of Israel. Every place that the sole of your foot will tread upon I have given you, as I said to Moses. From the wilderness and this Lebanon as far as the great river, the River Euphrates, all the land of the Hittites, and to the Great Sea toward the going down of the sun, shall be your territory. No man shall be able to stand before you all the days of your life; as I was with Moses, so I will be with you. I will not leave you nor forsake you. Be strong and of good courage, for to this people you shall divide as an inheritance the land which I swore to their fathers to give them. Only be strong and very courageous, that you may observe to do according to all the law which Moses My servant commanded you; do not turn from it to the right hand or to the left, that you may prosper wherever you go. This Book of the Law shall not depart from

your mouth, but you shall meditate in it day and night, that you may observe to do according to all that is written in it. For then you will make your way prosperous, and then you will have good success. Have I not commanded you? Be strong and of good courage; do not be afraid, nor be dismayed, for the LORD your God is with you wherever you go." - Joshua 1:2-9

In God we Trust!
by Faith, Love, Justice & Peace
Shawna Ranae
President | CEO
Website Treeoflifegroup.com
Gloryofzion.com
Goldenoilwealthadvisors.com

About Shawna Ranae

Shawna Ranae is the CEO of a fully credited and licensed Insurance Brokerage Firm specializing in varies products such as Life & Health Insurance, Term & Whole Life | Retirement | Indexed UL's | IRAs | 401k | Procurement | Annuities | Group Coverage | 403b, 457 | Medicare | Independent | Accidental with Disability | Living Benefit Products and so much more.

Shawna is well known to her clients as a Strategic Business Strategist and a Generational Investor, Financial & Estate Planning, Visionary, Philanthropist, Business of Zion Partner, Scribial Writer and Business Developer, Life Coach, Motivational Speaker, Inventor (Patent), Mentor, Advanced Marketing Specialist, Bible Enthusiast, Mother, Entrepreneur and most important a Servant for Jesus Christ.

Shawna has a wide spread educational background, including a Bachelor's degree in Finance and Business.

Shawna Ranae
President | CEO | Visionary
Tree of Life Group, Inc. | TreeOfLifeGroup.com
Golden Oil Wealth Advisors |
GoldenOilWealthAdvisors.com
GoldenWheat.org | GoldenWheat.org

Scriptural Structures We Support
Israel | GZI-Israel.org | *Genesis 12:3, Psalms 122:6*
Glory of Zion | GloryOfZion.org
Elijah Foundation | ElijahFoundationFSM.com
Zion Oil & Gas | ZionOil.com

Working with Military Veterans Transitioning into Civilian Life

Lefford Fate has led, mentored, and served thousands of military members and their families during his 31 years in the United States Air Force.

Since retiring from the military, he has been the program director for the geriatric outpatient mental health program, deputy Director for Health Services, SC Department of Corrections, and now the Director Support Services, City of Sumter.

Conversation with Lefford Fate

Lefford, give us a snapshot of what has brought you to this point in your life and why your heart and passion is for helping veterans transitioning into civilian life

Lefford Fate: Alright, well thank you for this opportunity, I spent 31 years in the United States Air Force. I retired as the command chief of the 20th Fighter Wing, uh, for the folks that are not in the military, that's the senior enlisted advisor for 5,000 airmen and about 22,000 people that are family members. That was my job. What got me into this field is, I've been a mental health professional since the early 90's, and one of my jobs was working with active duty military, many of those people were struggling based on transitions and deployments and moving in and out of the military. I have a special place in my heart to try and help them because I lost friends in the military due to suicide and PTSD, depression and anxiety. I wanted to help, so when I got out of the military, I worked as a program director for Geriatric Mental Health Facility, and I saw more people struggling with mental illness YEARS after transitioning out of the military. It didn't seem like they were getting the help that they needed and I needed it to do something.

I would suspect someone who is about to be deployed while they're transitioning from being in the United States to being deployed somewhere overseas and then coming back is a transition. Then, of course, transitioning from military life to civilian life, did you see different stages like that? What are the different ways that people need to be supported and encouraged?

Lefford Fate: I remember deploying to Iraq, and I was there for about six months transitioning back home from a war zone back into my family lifestyle where my wife and children have lived their life without me and me transitioning back in. That was traumatic for them AND for me. So many different types of transitions could cause issues if you're not properly prepared for it.

It's interesting that you said, "properly prepared" because if these men and women that are being in these times of transition in active duty or transitioning to civilian life if you do not properly prepare mentally, ahead of time, is that a major part of the battle? Having someone that has been there and done that like yourself and that can work with someone and help prepare them and work with them before, during and after, I would suspect is a huge opportunity.

Lefford Fate: I actually think that's probably the number one thing that a person can do, or a leader can do for their people. A big part of resiliency is understanding expectation management. If you deploy and you expect everything to be rainbows and Unicorns while downrange, and it's not, that's going to be a problem, but if you know when you go, it's going to be difficult. It's going to be tough. You're going to be gone for a certain amount of time. Then you can prepare yourself mentally, physically, and spiritually, coming back home, understanding that when you get back, your family's been doing well enough without you. They love you. They don't necessarily need you for day to day life. Understanding that you must integrate back into that family unit again. That is what helps you be resilient. Understanding what you're getting into and having somebody there that can come alongside you and walk along that path. That's very helpful. I will promise you this. I've seen domestic violence. I've seen divorce, I've seen abuse of substances like alcohol and all kinds of things strictly based on people coming back into the household, not expecting what they receive when they get there,

They must prepare for the next 90 days of their life in this civilian life of transition. So, understand what to expect, it's setting those expectations and then planning on how their responses need to be. Not reactions.

Lefford Fate: Exactly, if we can get people to understand that, we can save lives there. There are a lot of numbers you hear from 20 to 22 veterans commit suicide every day. Then 55 percent of the population that are first responders, whether it's police, whether it's military, first responders, they are dealing with divorce or have been divorced. Much of that is because there's poor expectation. They've not planned where they can respond versus react. If we could get in front of that, we could save lives and marriages.

It's not even like. I think we're talking about something that's bigger than just this topic of "transition." We're talking about saving a life, and it reminds me of that story of the GRANDPA and the grandson walking down the beach, and he's throwing those starfish back in. He says, "hey, this is a living creature. Let's save this one and save this one". So, the grandson says, "Grandpa, there's millions... you can't save them all... what's it matter? You're not going to be able to get to them all." Then the Grandpa says, "well, it makes a difference to this one right here. And it makes a difference to this one right here." So, you've got to look at the one right in front of you. So, if you can do some things to save that life, well, that's a significant impact.

Lefford Fate: I lost a really good friend, not much more than a year ago, because he did not transition well. He was a high-ranking officer in the United States Air Force. He deployed numerous times. He lost men and women in combat. He did not feel that he can get help. So, he took it all on himself. He self-medicated, he didn't go to a psychiatrist or a psychologist because he felt that he would be kicked out of the military, couldn't deploy, or she was fearful for himself and he died at 53 years old... all from building things up in his own mind that may or may not have been the case to begin with. You must understand where you can get help, that you don't have to do it alone, that you don't have to suck it up because that's one of the things that a lot, especially men, but women do it too in the military. However, you need to be strong enough to get help too.

I remember there was a great friend of mine; he was probably one of the sharpest non-commissioned officers that I met in my life and his grandfather who raised him because his father was out of the picture. He raised him with, took ill and my friend was devastated, and he came to me, said, you know, I'm going to make Chief Master Sergeant. All I need to do is stick around, but they want me to go overseas for four years. My grandfather needs me. So, it was a tough choice for my friend, we talked about his decision. He said you know what? This man stood in the gap for me when I couldn't take care of myself and so I'm going to stay. He decided to get out of the military. He took a civilian job on base. He remained there with his grandfather who lived another two years; but those two years were two of the best years of my friend's life and two of the best years of his grandfather's life as well. My friend is happy, successful, and he taught his son what it meant to love and to care for the people that care about by living it out! So, all of this came from a discussion about "what is your expectation?" If he took that assignment, you go off and make Chief, but you are not happy. What value is it to a man to earn all the riches in the world, but lose his soul or to lose somebody that he loved? Can you imagine what he would have felt like if his grandfather would've passed and he was gone? However, giving up a portion of his dream, what did he get from it? He got his grandfather. He got a great life, and he taught his son some lifelong lessons.

When you're describing that, it makes me think of his legacy, he was building a legacy in that period of time by giving up something. He took one step back and got 10 steps forward.

Lefford Fate: Exactly. You know, I learned that from Don Green who is the Executive Director of the Napoleon Hill Foundation. I was talking to him and said, "you know, I want to leave a legacy." He said, "leaving a legacy is great, but LIVE your legacy" I will never forget that. Live your legacy. So, this is what my friend did. Steve did that!

Lefford, you've been talking about working with some of these men and women that are in transition. So, I wonder if it is accurate to say that the men or women in the military that need help talking through & working through transition, if that's only 50 percent of the equation. The other 50 percent is their family on the other side. So, if someone like yourself is

*working with, talking through some of these expectations -
that that same kind of conversations needs to be had with the
family members, right? Talk a little bit about how working
with the family that they're coming back to, is a big piece of
this equation for success.*

Lefford Fate: Well, one of the things that we're doing is
working with families before the deployment, talking about
what's going to go on during that time that they're gone away,
explaining what they are going to be dealing with when
they're away. They may not get a phone call for a while.
Right? So, there's expectation management there. Then, this is
what's going to happen right before they come back, and these
are some of the things that they've been dealing with. We
work with the family members while the spouse is gone and
we're also working with the deployed airmen, and we also
worked with soldiers and sailors also. This is what you can
expect when you get back, so there are actual processes that
are out there that can be used. One of the concerns that I have,
it's voluntary, and sometimes people believe "I got this. I don't
need help, I don't need assistance." The problem that I see
with that is you cannot see the picture when you're in the
frame and so awareness of the fact that these are some things
that can happen if you don't get this help, those are the things
that we can do because it, it works. Period. When people are
prepared for what they're going to expect, it prepares them
like nothing else.

*You mentioned the example of your friend that turned out
in a negative result. Can you explain a situation or two where
you were working with a family and working with someone in*

transition, and things just went better than how they could have?

Lefford Fate: Well, if you could see me now. I've got this great smile on my face because there's this one young airman who was planning on sending his family back home because they came to Shaw Air Force base and they were struggling. He deployed right before he came over and they weren't doing well. They were going to give it up. They're just going to say, know "this is over." So, we talked about "what do you need from him? What do you need from her?" This conversation happened separately I talked to the wife by herself, and I talked to the husband by himself and then brought them back together and asked: "what would it look like if you guys can have a great relationship in 90 days?" They talked about how good it would be and how to make that happen. Now, I don't know if this is the reason why, but this young man just was awarded one of the 12 Outstanding Airmen of the Air Force. This is a big deal. He was promoted three times. He's going to be a Master Sergeant. He re-enlisted, he and his wife have had another child, and they're extremely happy....and it's all because of expectation management.

It seems like the ripple effect, you feel a pebble into a pond, and it just ripples outward. It doesn't only impact right where the pebble landed. So, you were working with mindset and expectations in one specific area, and that got him fine-tuning his approach to many things, and I would submit to you that he then started following those same types of thought processes and expectation management and personal development in many areas of his life.

Lefford Fate: Exactly. It's like the saying: "how you do anything is how you do everything." Also, the cool thing about it is; honestly, I watched this guy, he just did a Facebook live video where he's mentoring other young people. So, it's not just something where you do it yourself, and it just stops there. It's more like being a river versus a reservoir. This guy is reaching out and trying to help other people- it's amazing how just having somebody step into your life and, and passing on information - if you can help somebody understand that how something they can go a lot further and they will pass that value on, I can promise you that he or she will almost always pass the values on.

Well, there's that word again, that legacy, with your work with him and impact with him. There's no way to know this. However, what if you hadn't come into his life, he might have been fine...but because of this new mindset, not only did he get those promotions and life-improvements but then he did something else which I think is just extraordinary. He's now giving back and paying it forward and serving other people. So now Lefford Fate is having a legacy "ripple-effect" into people that you don't even know because of him. We don't know what kind of significant impact that we can have in people's lives!

Lefford Fate: Exactly. Exactly. And you know, there was a tech sergeant, John Gunther back in 1986 was that person for me! It was just like "The Tale of Two Cities" It was the best of times and the worst of times. On 18, March 1986, my first son was born... on March fourth, 1986. My mother died, and I very nearly lost myself, if not for a guy by the name of Technical Sergeant John Gunther who thought better of me.

He saw the pain in me, but he also saw me in the pain! He was there for me, and he talked to me. He wasn't my best friend, some of the stuff you said was kind of harsh, but he did not let me fall when he could have easily. So, I think back, and it's funny how the circle happened. He was one of the 12 Outstanding Airman of the Air Force. He saved me. I was able to help save somebody else who ended up being one of the 12 Outstanding Airman of the Air Force.

Wow. You talk about a legacy! You have told him that over and over, correct?

Lefford Fate: You know what? This is the crazy part. When I said it just now, that was the first time I recognized that. Right there.

What an opportunity you must speak a positive word and blessing into this man's life when you do call him up or get together and explain the legacy that he poured into your life and show him that it's not stopping. That's amazing.

Lefford Fate: Well, I thanked him, and Chief Retired Gunther is still out there. We're, we're great friends. He's a mentor of mine. However, I did not tell him this story.... yet!

Well, what a wonderful epiphany moment. If someone is impacted by your message and your impact and legacy, the things we've been talking about and he or she wonders if you can help them too, what's the best way that someone can reach out to you in a confidential manner?

Lefford Fate: Well, the best way is to look me up is at leffordfate.com and I can reach out to you. I'm giving you my direct number. As I said, I have lost friends in the military because somebody was not there for them. I don't want anybody to have to feel that way. So, if you reach out to me, I will answer. I will get you to somebody that has the help and as far as coaching and figuring out what you want, who you are, and to be able to ask the right questions. Because if we get ready, we can handle anything, and I'd love to be able to come alongside somebody and help them get through because transitions are real, but we could get through them if we prepare!

About Lefford Fate

Professionally, I've led, mentored, and served thousands of military members and their families during my 31 years in the United States Air Force. Since retiring from the military, I have been the program director for the geriatric outpatient mental health program, deputy Director for Health Services, SC Department of Corrections, and now the Director Support Services, City of Sumter.

I am a husband, father, and grandfather, so I know it is not always easy to juggle our list of daily responsibilities. This makes it even more important to have a structured, practical plan in place to avoid becoming overwhelmed. I hold a Master's degree in Human Relations and a Bachelor's degree in Social Psychology. Modeling the core values of Integrity first, Service before self and Excellence in all I do. I believe there is a "why" for everyone; that each of us was created with the potential to achieve greatness, to make a difference in the world, to add value to others, and as a result, experience a full and rewarding life. For over 30 years, my purpose was to defend our nation, and now that purpose is helping people discover their life's purpose and grow to their full potential.

You have met your Fate; let's walk into your destiny.

WEBSITE
LeffordFate.com

PHONE
(850) 319-8070

Make $1K per Day with Smartphone Video

What's more important, the message or the machine? It's a question Brandy Sales usually asks at the beginning of his presentations and workshops. Several entrepreneurs working with Brandy in 2014 inspired him to seriously consider the question after many of them admitted that they wanted to use video to help grow their business but could not afford traditional video production. His clients, and a Bentley commercial shot on an iPhone 5, became the catalyst for Brandy, a four-time international Telly award-winning video producer, to start creating videos with his smartphone.

Once he figured out the process and system, he took the concept to youth programs and taught teens how to produce everything on their phone or iPads. As the founder of BrandySales.com based in Burlington, Massachusetts, Brandy not only produces award-winning videos, he specializes in teaching business owners video marketing as a speaker and video production coach. By combining his professional video production expertise with the DIY techniques he developed for smartphone video production, he teaches hundreds of entrepreneurs and business owners how to create powerful, effective smartphone videos that grow their business. Brandy has helped entrepreneurs worldwide generate thousands of leads and sales through his speaking engagements, on-site trainings and workshops, two-day Smartphone Video Camp and self-guided virtual Smartphone Video School.

Conversation with Brandy Sales

How are you helping entrepreneurs grow their business with video?

Brandy Sales: My business is all about simplifying the "do it yourself" video production process, and the goal is to help my clients add up to $1K per day with video production, which we've seen some of our clients do using our techniques.

What do you mean by $1K per day?

Brandy Sales: We're looking for business owners who already have a marketing plan in place or they have a really strong message. By adding video, they add sales to their already growing business. One client used our DIY techniques and decided to start doing one Facebook live video a week. She sells a product that's $7,000 and every single time that she does a Facebook live video she sells at least one product. She's seen that happen for the last three months consistently, which for her is adding $1,000 per day by doing one Facebook live video for the last three months.

Why do you focus on video?

Brandy Sales: I lost my mom six years ago. We did video together when I was 12. We produced 100 television shows for the town of Burlington, Massachusetts and the only video of her I have is from 1997 when she interviewed me on our very last show together. That's the video I hold onto. I can't stand how I look but it doesn't matter. My mom is there and that's what matters. I show it to my kids and that is more important to me than anything. That's really what video comes down to me. It comes down to leaving a legacy. Any video I produce professionally, any video that I help somebody create on their own, it's got to come down to the legacy that you want to leave.

What inspired you to focus on smartphone video production in particular and what are the advantages of it compared to traditional video production?

Brandy Sales: What's more important, the message or the machine? It's a question I usually start out my talks with and that's really what it comes down to for me. In 2014, I was working with many women entrepreneurs who were saying "I want to do more videos but I can't afford [traditional production]." Then I see this Bentley commercial that was shot on an iPhone 5 and it totally blew my mind. Once I figured out the process and system, that's when I started teaching smartphone video to business owners. I basically took what I was doing in the professional video production world and blended it with DIY the techniques to make it easier for the business owner to learn and do.

What's your advice for entrepreneurs and executives who don't like to be in front of the camera?

Brandy Sales: I often hear "I don't like to be in front of the camera" or "I don't have anything to say," so instead I ask, "What do you have to show?" People like to watch things. People like to listen to things too but if you're really scared to be in front of the camera, try showing something instead.

Write a script where we only hear your voice and then show different images to help tell your story.

What are other fears or common myths about smartphone video production?

Brandy Sales: The tech is too complicated. When you look at the tech it comes down to practice, practice and more practice. When you look at the equipment it comes down to six areas of equipment, which I break down for my clients.

For the people that don't know where to start I would say, make an introductory video. Tell people who you are, what you do and how to contact you. We do these intro videos in our workshops and if you can explain on camera about what you do then that tells me right away that you know your business. If you don't know your business and can't speak about it, it's going to be really hard to make any type of video, professional or do it yourself.

Another misconception is time. Sometimes people don't think it's worth it but if you put in four hours of time making videos for your brand and share it with your audience you're saving yourself time in the long run because your videos are working for you 24 hours a day and seven days a week. You're creating the relationships that you need in order to sell more and build more engagement with your community.

What are the six categories of equipment that can get business owners started with smartphone video?

Brandy Sales: You need to have a camera, which is your smartphone. You need stabilizers like a [standing] tripod or a handheld tripod. Gimbals are another kind of stabilizer that works well for travel agents or real estate agents who want to do tours of places. You also need microphones, lighting, mounts, and then finally, memory and storage. iPhone users run out of space often and there are small fixes like a USB stick that goes into the bottom of your phone that you can record directly to and then transfer to your computer right away. For Android systems, micro SD cards can expand your memory and you can record hours of video without a problem.

Once you have the right equipment, what are some of the common mistakes that people make in regards to technique?

Brandy Sales: Shooting with your back to a window is a common mistake. Some other mistakes would be to buy the cheapest microphone possible. Another common thing I see is on Facebook live videos is that people don't know where to look. They look at themselves on their phone screen instead of looking right at the camera. Connecting with your audience is very important and shifty eyes, is not a good thing!

What are some of the common objections you get from business owners when it comes to investing in video whether it's doing it themselves or hiring someone?

Brandy Sales: Being in front of the camera is the biggest and that simply takes a conversation about how you can show your brand without sitting in front of the camera. The other one is "I don't like my voice on camera." You can hire someone to do a voiceover for you for $5 on fiverr.com. The third one is not enough time and in that case, you can hire a professional production team and get it done fairly quickly but you're going to spend anywhere between $1,500 to $5,000 on a professional video. So, I say invest the time in learning how to do videos on your own. Maybe the DIY videos compliment that one professional video you have. Now you have the ability to make any other type of video you want. If you want to do training videos, you can do that on your phone. There's no reason to hire a videographer and spend $3,000 on shooting training videos. You can shoot your own training videos on your phone for a $200 investment in equipment and two days with me learning the tools and techniques. You get the same system I use for my professional productions; the only difference is that I substitute in the equipment that makes sense for consumers.

You've helped raised a lot of money for non-profit organizations using video marketing. Tell us about that.

Brandy Sales: Yes, we've helped many non-profit organizations nationwide raise $75 million over two years. We've worked with The Dimock Center in Boston, one of the oldest community health centers in the country; Hoodfit, a community organization in Boston that focuses on mind, body and spirit; Boston Athletic Association; Boston Public Schools and MassHousing to name a few. It's the same system applied to my non-profit clients. I focus on building the connection with audiences through the story lines, but we also identify their main goal and how they want people to feel after they watch the video. I was on set last week where I was literally sharing tears with a mom that is trying to get reconnected with her kids after a drug addiction. I asked the organization "What do you want people to feel after they watch this video?" and they said we want the audience to be in tears.

We did a campaign for The Dimock Center in partnership with [Massachusetts] Governor Charlie Baker and Attorney General Maura Healey about the opioid epidemic where we collected smartphone videos from around the state from parents with kids who have either passed away or who are struggling with opioid addition. We opened the video with their smartphone videos. I could have shot that on a $10,000 camera but we had them shoot their own stories on their smartphones. The smartphone videos get the feeling across just the same.

If business owners wanted to learn how to do their own videos what should they look for to make sure they're investing in the right trainer?

Brandy Sales: Ask them to take you through their process. That is going to separate the trainers from the video professionals who try to make some money on the side by teaching people. If they can explain it to you simply, it's probably going to be a good fit for you.

How can people find out more about Brandy Sales and how to get involved with what you're doing?

Brandy Sales: BrandySales.com has information about my smartphone video talks, trainings and workshops, as well as free tips at the blog. Details for my upcoming Smartphone Video Camps are available at SmartPhoneVideoCamp.net.

About Brandy Sales

Brandy Sales is a four-time international Telly award-winning video producer, speaker and video production coach. He is also the president and founder of WeCast, an 8-week application-based iPad video production program for children ages seven to 13. Brandy posted his first video to a website in 1999. In 2013, he created a video production company that was able to help raise $75 million for non-profit organizations throughout the United States. Some of his notable speaking engagements include the National Women's Business Conference, Rotary International, Be a Real Estate Star, Video Producers of the Future Night with the Boston Celtics and the Self-Employment in the Arts Conference. He has been featured in *Boston Voyager Magazine* and the *Burlington Union*, and appeared on several business podcasts including Market

Your Biz Better, Computer Business Marketing Show and Thrive. As the founder of BrandySales.com, he specializes in teaching business owners how to create powerful, effective smartphone videos that grow their business.

BUSINESS NAME
Brandy Sales – Video Expert and Coach

WEBSITE
BrandySales.com/

EMAIL
brandy@brandysales.com

FACEBOOK
Facebook.com/BrandySalesVideo

LINKEDIN
LinkedIn.com/in/BrandySales/

TWITTER
Twitter.com/Brandy_Sales

www.ingramcontent.com/pod-product-compliance
Lightning Source LLC
Chambersburg PA
CBHW060604200326

41521CB00007B/655